BIG BOOK OF KNITTED MITTENS

JORID LINVIK'S

Big book of

KNITTED MITTENS

45 DISTINCTIVE SCANDINAVIAN PATTERNS

BY JORID LINVIK

TS

TRAFALGAR SQUARE
North Pomfret, Vermont

First published in the United States of America
in 2016 by
Trafalgar Square Books
North Pomfret, Vermont 05053

Originally published in Norwegian as *Den store votteboka*

ISBN: 978-1-57076-786-9

Library of Congress Control Number: 2016940014

INTERIOR DESIGN: Johanne Hjorthol
OUTDOOR PHOTOS: Evy Andersen
TRANSLATION: Carol Huebscher Rhoades

Printed in China
10 9 8 7 6 5 4 3 2

CONTENTS

PREFACE

When I was a little girl, I received a pair of mittens my aunt had knitted for me. They were blue and white with bird motifs. I was so happy! At that time, during the 1960s, it wasn't very common to have garments with picture motifs.

These fine mittens were worn all winter.

But eventually one day one of the mittens disappeared! By then my aunt's knitting pattern had also disappeared. The remaining mitten was so felted together that it couldn't be used as a pattern for some new mittens, but I saved it for many years.

In 2007, I came across a pattern for the same mittens. Now I could finally have a new pair of bird mittens! Unfortunately, there was no one who had the time to knit mittens for me, and I didn't understand how to work the pattern. It looked altogether too complicated for me, and I had hardly any knitting experience.

I went ahead anyway and worked day and night on my bird mittens. Many stitches were ripped out and many swear words unleashed during the process, as well as several telephone conversations had with my mother, who was very supportive.

And, eventually, after lots of trial and error, the mittens were finished! I had cracked the code and was well on my way to successful mitten knitting. I found out it is both fun and easy to knit mittens, once you have a little practice. If you have a basic pattern, the possibilities are endless. I started designing my own patterns and sharing them, and after a while there were more and more people who wanted to buy patterns from me. I started a little web store, Jorid's Pattern Shop, on the internet (at Ravelry.com) and now you can find a number of my mitten patterns there, as well as designs for other knitted garments such as socks and hats.

So you won't be as discouraged as I was at the beginning, all of my patterns have instructions that are as clear and well-written as I could make them. I also recommend that you read the introduction with tips and information about yarn and sizing. That way you might not have to rip out quite as many stitches as I did.

It may still be a bit of a struggle to start with, but once you get the hang of knitting mittens, it's like a game. And a few mistakes are all right, as long as you try your best and like the result—"love covers a multitude of sins," as they say!

BODØ, AUGUST 2015
Jorid Linvik

BASIC KNITTING TIPS

Ribbing

Ribbing should be worked fairly firmly—it can often end up looser than desired—but should remain elastic. A good rule of thumb is to work the ribbing with needles one size smaller than the needles used for the rest of the mitten. Another option is to work the purl stitches, or even all the stitches, as twisted stitches.

Dominant Color

Usually a pattern design has a well-defined motif set against a background. For example, when you look at the Cat mittens on page 26, the cat is the motif—the yarn used for the cat is the "pattern" yarn, or contrast color. The rest of the mitten is worked using the "background" yarn, or main color.

A pattern motif will show most clearly when the pattern color is held so it comes under the background color strand on the back of the piece. It's very important for the colors to be held this way in relation to each other through the whole pattern, so the knitting will be even.

If you forget and start holding the yarns the other way around partway through the knitting, it will show as an uneven section with a different look.

Some knitters hold one strand on their left forefinger and the other strand in their right hand or on the right forefinger. The yarn held in the left hand will come under the other strand on the wrong side of the knitting—this should be the pattern yarn or contrast color of the pattern. If you hold both colors in your left hand, the strand held further down your finger should be the pattern color, as it will lie under the other strand.

The Wrong Side

In order to produce evenly knitted mittens, make sure the yarn strands lie evenly and smoothly on the wrong side throughout. If you pull on the strands too hard when changing colors, the fabric will be pulled in across the width. Strands that are too loose will also negatively affect the look and sizing of the mittens.

One tip is to stretch the strands and stitches across the width every time you change needles. Take a peek at the wrong side to make sure the strands or "floats" lie smooth and flat.

Long Floats

It can be challenging to have long floats between color changes and it is uncomfortable to have long strands on the inside of your mittens. To avoid long floats, twist the colors around each other every 5-6 stitches. Don't forget to stretch the piece to make sure the piece doesn't pull in.

Joining Yarn

Sometimes you'll run out of yarn in the middle of a row and need to attach

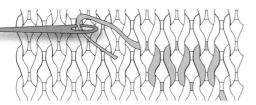

Follow the structure of the knit stitches when embroidering with another color.

a new ball of yarn. You can knot the yarn ends (leaving ends long enough to weave in later) and knit so that the knot lies on the wrong side. When the item is finished, you can untie the knot(s) and weave in the yarn ends.

Duplicate Stitch Embroidery

Some designs in this book have motifs with a few stitches that should be embroidered—in a different color than that used for knitting the mitten.

You can also use duplicate stitch to correct an error in a color pattern after you've finished knitting the piece, and initials and dates can be added in duplicate stitch on the finished mittens to make them more personal.

Uneven Yarn

If you find knots, visible joins, or any other unevenness in your yarns, I recommend that you cut the yarn and join it as described above. If you don't eliminate the knots and bad joins, you will only be irritated later on!

Weaving in Ends

All yarn ends must be securely woven in on the wrong side of the mittens with a tapestry needle. Check to make sure the ends are woven in on the wrong side only and don't show through on the right side.

Weave in ends by sewing them for 1½-2 in / 4-5 cm along the knitting, working in and out through the tops of the stitches or through the strands between stitches. Turn and sew back until a little past the point where you started. Now, bring the needle a couple of times through the same strand that you have been sewing with. Make sure the yarn lies smoothly and doesn't pull in when you trim it.

Sometimes there will be a little hole in the knitting at the base of the thumb. You can tighten up the hole on the wrong side by using the end of the thumb yarn to pull its edges together *at the same time* as you weave in the ends. Never tie knots unless you're planning to undo them later and weave in the ends instead.

Seaming the Top

Some of the mittens in this book are joined at the top with Kitchener stitch. This method produces a smooth finish and makes the mitten more rounded at the top.

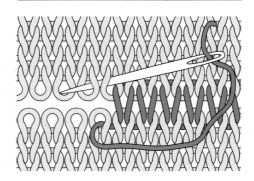

Kitchener stitch.

YARN

All the mittens in this book have been knitted with classic, good-quality yarns that are easy to find. For the best possible results, it's important to use yarn that is appropriate for the project you want to knit. If you're working a pattern with two or more colors, it's also important to find colors that contrast well, so the motifs on the mittens will show clearly.

Wool Yarn

Wool is an excellent fiber for pattern knitting—wool yarn has a lot of elasticity, so a garment made with it will drape nicely and fit well. Loosely plied yarn has less elasticity than well-twisted yarn; a garment made with it will be soft but dense. Mittens knitted in wool will stay warm even when wet, and after you wear them for a while, they'll conform to the shape of your hands.

Mittens knitted with a regular wool yarn will also felt a little on the palms if they're used as work or ski mittens. Some think this is a charming look that makes the mittens extra personal. If the yarn is "superwash," the mittens will be stronger, can be machine-washed, and won't felt with use.

Alpaca Yarn

Alpaca fiber is even more warming than wool. Pattern-knitted mittens made with alpaca yarn will keep the hands warm on even the coldest winter day, but they won't hold that warmth if they get wet. Alpaca is really nice for pattern knitting, but you do have to knit more carefully because alpaca lacks wool's elasticity. Alpaca is best for smooth mittens that won't be used for sports or work, since they won't be especially durable.

Other Fibers

If you are allergic to wool or don't want to use animal products, there are still many options to choose from. You can get good knitting results from acrylic, soft cotton, bamboo, or polyamide. Try out these fibers by knitting gauge swatches before you embark on a whole mitten.

KNITTING NEEDLES AND SIZES

Needles

In Scandinavia, mittens are usually worked with a total of 5 double-pointed needles. The needle size corresponds to the diameter of the needle and is given in millimeters (mm). U.S. knitting needles are numbered differently and there is not always an exact match for a millimeter size. In U.S. sizes, the smaller the size number, the smaller the needle.

When you buy needles, it's important to choose a needle size appropriate for the yarn and pattern you'll be using. Needle lengths are measured in inches or centimeters. Double-pointed needles (dpn) for socks are usually 6–8 in / 15–20 cm long, which is also a perfect length for mittens.

Knitting needles are made from a wide variety of materials, including aluminum, wood, bamboo, and carbon. It can take a while to figure out which needles are just right for you. Some knitters prefer heavy, smooth metal needles while others like lighter bamboo needles.

Gauge

The band around a ball of yarn indicates the recommended gauge for that yarn by listing the number of stitches in 4 in / 10 cm.

NOTE: When you are knitting a pattern with two colors, the gauge will be tighter than with only one color. As a general rule of thumb, you will need 2 stitches more for every 4 in / 10 cm than will be given on the ball band. For example, if the ball band recommends 22 sts = 4 in / 10 cm with needles that are U.S. size 2.5 / 3 mm, there will be 24 sts in 4 in / 10 cm for two-color stranded knitting with the same needle size.

Some people knit loosely while others knit tightly, and not everyone will achieve the gauge as given in the pattern or on the yarn ball band. For that reason, you should always make a gauge swatch and measure it out. If the swatch is too large, then you should switch to smaller needles, and if the swatch is too small, try larger needles. After you have gained some knitting experience, it will be easier to estimate the right needle size for the desired results.

How Do You Get the Right Size?

All the mittens in this book can be knitted in a variety of sizes following the same pattern.

The secret lies in the choice of yarn and the needle size, which, when combined well, will give you the gauge appropriate for the desired size. The size of the finished mitten is determined by the circumference of the hand as measured above the thumb. The length of the mitten should be in proportion to the circumference and suitable for the size. To easily determine the circumference of a mitten, lay the mitten flat on a table and measure the width just above the thumb; then multiply by 2.

It is not always easy to get the exact measurements of a finished mitten, since knitting is elastic. Luckily, that elasticity allows some flexibility in sizing and fit. You may find that after a while your mittens fit perfectly, even though they originally seemed too tight or too loose.

Mittens with 48 stitches in a round, child-size mittens

SIZE	CIRCUMFERENCE	GAUGE
0-2 years	4¾-5¼ in / 12-13 cm	34 sts = 4 in / 10 cm
3-4 years	5¾ in / 14.5 cm	33 sts = 4 in / 10 cm
5-7 years	6 in / 15 cm	32 sts = 4 in / 10 cm
7-10 years	6¾ in / 17 cm	28 sts = 4 in / 10 cm
10-12 years	7 in / 18 cm	25 sts = 4 in / 10 cm

LITTLE SQUIRREL, P. 117

CALF, P. 146

LITTLE RABBIT, P. 30

LITTLE FOX, P. 106

ROE DEER FAWN, P. 114

LITTLE LAMB, P. 158

LITTLE BIRD, P. 58

TIGER CUB, P. 194

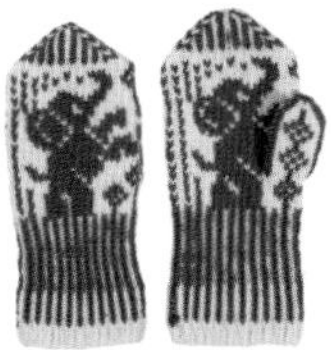

BABY ELEPHANT, P. 203

Mittens with 60 stitches in a round, teen- and adult-size mittens

SIZE	CIRCUMFERENCE	GAUGE
10-12 years	7 in / 18 cm	33 sts = 4 in / 10 cm
12-16 years/ Women's small	7½ in / 19 cm	31 sts = 4 in / 10 cm
Women's medium	8 in / 20 cm	30 sts = 4 in / 10 cm
Men's small/ Women's large	8¼ in / 21 cm	29 sts = 4 in / 10 cm
Men's medium	8¾ in / 22 cm	28 sts = 4 in / 10 cm
Men's large	9 in / 22.5 cm	27 sts = 4 in / 10 cm

GIRAFFE, P. 197

MOTHER SQUIRREL,
P. 120

TIDDELY POM,
P. 184

LET'S ROCK, P. 172

CAT MITTENS,
P. 26

SANDRA SALAMANDER,
P.124

PTARMIGAN, P. 55

NORTH POLE,
P. 132

DOG MITTENS,
P.34

ANGEL MITTENS,
P. 164

BIRD MITTENS,
P. 48

POODLE MITTENS,
P. 38

FISHERMAN'S FRIEND, P. 175

DANCING FROGS, P. 124

HORSE, P. 138

JORID'S CHRISTMAS HEARTS, P. 82

CAT AND MOUSE, P. 42

TANGO ELEPHANT, P. 200

REINDEER, P. 154

Mittens with 64 stitches in a round, teen- and adult-size mittens

SIZE	CIRCUMFERENCE	GAUGE
10-12 years	7 in / 18 cm	34 sts = 4 in / 10 cm
12-16 years/ Women's small	7½ in / 19 cm	33 sts = 4 in / 10 cm
Women's medium	8 in / 20 cm	32 sts = 4 in / 10 cm
Men's small/ Women's large	8¼ in / 21 cm	31 sts = 4 in / 10 cm
Men's medium	8¾ in / 22 cm	29 sts = 4 in / 10 cm
Men's large	9 in / 22.5 cm	28 sts = 4 in / 10 cm

BRIDAL PAIR MITTENS,
P.178

FOX,
P.102

ZEBRA MITTENS,
P. 190

SHEEP MITTENS,
P. 150

SHIP AHOY,
P. 168

FLYING HEARTS,
P. 91

COW MITTENS,
P.142

SOUTH POLE,
P. 52

THE MOOSE HUNTERS,
P. 110

Mittens with 68 stitches in a round, adult sizes

SIZE	CIRCUMFERENCE	GAUGE
12-16 years/ Women's small	7½ in / 19 cm	33 sts = 4 in / 10 cm
Women's medium	8 in / 20 cm	32 sts = 4 in / 10 cm
Men's small/ Women's large	8¼ in / 21 cm	32 sts = 4 in / 10 cm
Men's medium	8¾ in / 22 cm	31 sts = 4 in / 10 cm
Men's large	9 in / 22.5 cm	30 sts = 4 in / 10 cm

KNOT, P. 94

NIGHT OWL,
P. 61

ICE CRYSTAL,
P. 85

TALLULAH'S HEART,
P. 88

Mittens Felted Down to the Desired Size

FLY AGARIC
MUSHROOMS, P. 73

BURNING LOVE,
P.66

DIAMOND COOKIES,
P. 70

WHITE TIGER,
P. 76

BASICS FOR KNITTING THE MITTENS IN THIS BOOK

The charts are read from right to left and from the bottom up—read in the same direction as the knitting. Each block on the chart corresponds to one stitch in the knitted fabric.

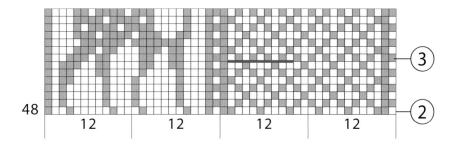

A number inside a circle refers to the corresponding number in the pattern.

The vertical lines marked on a chart divide the stitches by needle to make it easier to follow the pattern.

The numbers between the red lines indicate the stitch count for each needle. In this example, there are 12 sts on each of the four needles = 48 sts total.

Marking for the thumbhole: a dark horizontal line. The stitches on the row just above the dark line should be knitted with a smooth scrap yarn = the thumbhole row. Make sure the scrap yarn you use for this is a color that contrasts well with the pattern yarn so you can see the row later on.

For the thumbhole, work in pattern up to and including the stitch before the marker. Add in the scrap yarn and knit the thumbhole stitches (here 9 sts) above the dark line. Drop the scrap yarn and hide ends inside mitten. Slide the stitches just knitted in scrap yarn back to the left needle and work them in pattern following the chart.

Increases

All the increases are marked with a V on the charts. The marked square is a "new" stitch.

There are several methods for making increases. A common method is to "make one" (M1): lift the strand between two stitches and knit into the back loop of the strand. In two-color knitting, lift a strand the same color as for the increase stitch.

Or: Knit into the stitch below the previous or next stitch (left-lifted or right-lifted increase).

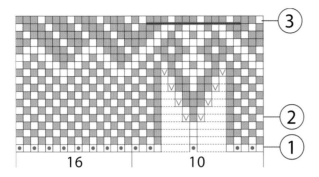

Shaping the Thumb Gusset

In some of the designs, extra stitches are added below the thumbhole to form a "thumb gusset." The number between the needle markers shows the number of stitches on the first round (1) on the chart, before the increases. On that round, there are no stitches on either side of the gusset. Begin increasing on the round marked 2 (number inside circle). In this example, you would knit 5 stitches and then increase 1 with the light yarn, knit 1 dark stitch, increase 1 with light, and then knit 4 more stitches to the end of the needle. Work subsequent increases the same way (with more stitches between increases each time, as shown on chart).

Decreases

All the decreases on the charts are marked with a diagonal line in the square where the decrease occurs. The slant of the slash indicates the direction of the decrease—to either the right or left.

Left-leaning Decrease Methods: Knit 2 stitches together through back loops (k2tog tbl), or slip 1, knit 1, pass slipped st over (sl 1, k1, psso), or (slip 1 st knitwise to right needle) 2 times, insert left needle left to right into the 2 sts and knit them together (ssk).

Right-leaning Decrease: Knit 2 together (k2tog).

For most of the mitten patterns, the left-leaning decreases occur on the left side of the mitten and the right-leaning decreases are on the right side. But some of the designs do have decreases worked the opposite way.

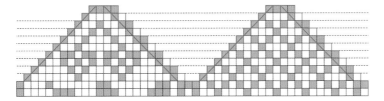

☑ Right-leaning Decrease
◩ Left-leaning Decrease

Knitting the Thumbs
All of the patterns show the front of the thumb on the right side of the chart and the back of the thumb on the left. Thumbs are worked in the round as for the mitten itself.

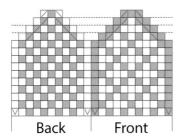

Back | Front

When the scrap yarn at the thumbhole is removed, it leaves an opening in the piece so that the thumb can be worked there.

Before you remove the scrap yarn, run one double-pointed needle through the stitches below the scrap yarn and other dpn in the stitches above the scrap yarn. Carefully remove the scrap yarn. Inserting the needles beforehand helps to insure that the stitches won't be dropped as you remove the scrap yarn.

Begin by working the stitches on the front of the thumb first. *At the same time,* increase at each side of the thumb as follows: On first side—knit a stitch into the last stitch of the mitten before you inserted the scrap yarn; on opposite side, increase by knitting into the first stitch after the scrap yarn. On the back of the thumb, increase by taking up into the stitch over the previous one taken up by the front.

The first round on the back of the thumb is worked into stitches that are actually "upside down." Be sure you knit into each stitch so that it lies correctly on the needle—this will make the thumb look as smooth and neat as possible.

ABBREVIATIONS

BO	bind off (= British cast off)
cm	centimeter(s)
CO	cast on
dpn	double-pointed needles
in	inch(es)
k	knit
k2tog	knit 2 together (right-leaning decrease)
m	meter(s)
M1	make 1 = lift strand between two sts and knit into back loop
mm	millimeter(s)
p	purl
rem	remain(s)(ing)
rnd(s)	rnd(s)
st(s)	stitch(es)
yd	yards
yo	yarnover

PATTERNS

CUDDLY ANIMALS

They make a tangled mess in the yarn basket. They set their sharp claws and teeth into your knitted garments and in an instant, hours of hard work disintegrate into bits of yarn. They trap you by settling down on your lap or legs or chest, and it's impossible to keep knitting or they'll take off with your balls of yarn.

But in spite of all that, we love our little friends! So here's a selection of mittens you can knit to honor some adorable cuddly animals. Just make sure the yarn doesn't get eaten while you work...

CAT MITTENS

MATERIALS
Yarn: CYCA #2 (sport/baby) BabySilk from Du Store Alpakka (80% baby alpaca, 20% silk; 145 yd/133 m / 50 g), Natural White #301 and Lilac #321
Needles: U.S. size 2.5 / 3 mm, set of 5 dpn

These two spritely cats spring high and low, meow and arch their backs. But after a little snack of fish, they'll settle down so you can work peacefully on your knitting.

It's easy to be comfortable wearing these cozy cat mittens, and they're perfect for anyone who likes cats. Why not knit them in colors that match the fur of a fuzzy little friend?

Instructions

With Natural White, CO 56 sts. Divide the sts evenly onto 4 dpn (= 14 sts per ndl). Join, being careful not to twist cast-on row.

1) Begin with the ribbing on Chart 1.

2) On the chart row marked with an encircled 2, increase 1 st on each needle = 60 sts total. Continue to end of Chart 1.

3) Now work Chart 2. The pattern is repeated twice around.

4) After completing the 6 rounds of Chart 2, work following the chart for the right- or left-hand mitten respectively (see pages 28-29).

5) **Thumbhole:** The thick line on the chart indicates the placement of the thumbhole. Knit the 11 sts for the thumb with smooth contrast color scrap yarn. Slide the sts back to the left needle and knit in pattern.

6) Continue following the chart up to the encircled 6, and shape top as shown on chart.

7) When 7 sts each remain on front and back, seam the sets of stitches with Kitchener stitch.

8) **Thumb:** Insert a dpn into the sts below the scrap yarn and another dpn into the sts above the scrap yarn. Remove the scrap yarn = 11 + 11 sts. On the first rnd of the thumb, increase to 26 sts total by picking up and knitting 2 sts at each side (see chart).

9) Work thumb to the encircled 9, and then shape top by decreasing as shown on chart.

10) When 6 sts remain, cut yarn and draw end through rem sts. Weave in all yarn ends neatly on WS.

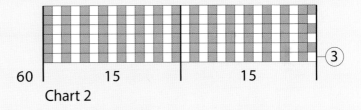

60 | 15 | 15 — ③

Chart 2

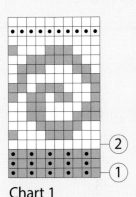

Chart 1

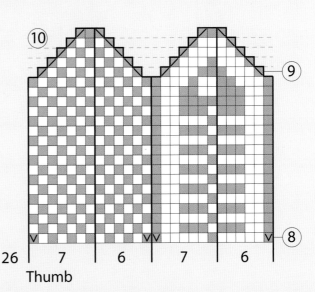

26 | 7 | 6 | 7 | 6 — ⑧

Thumb

▨	☐	Knit
⚫	⦁	Purl
Ⅴ		Increase 1 st
◿		Right-leaning decrease
◺		Left-leaning decrease

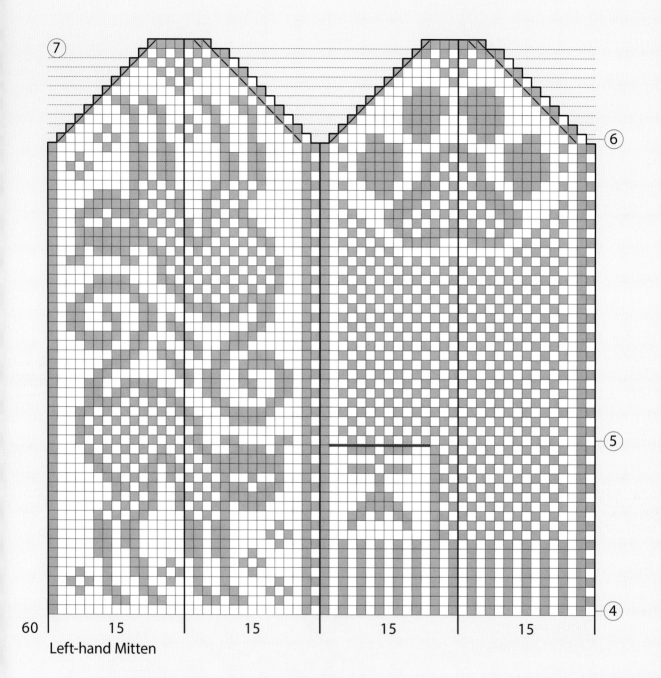

Left-hand Mitten

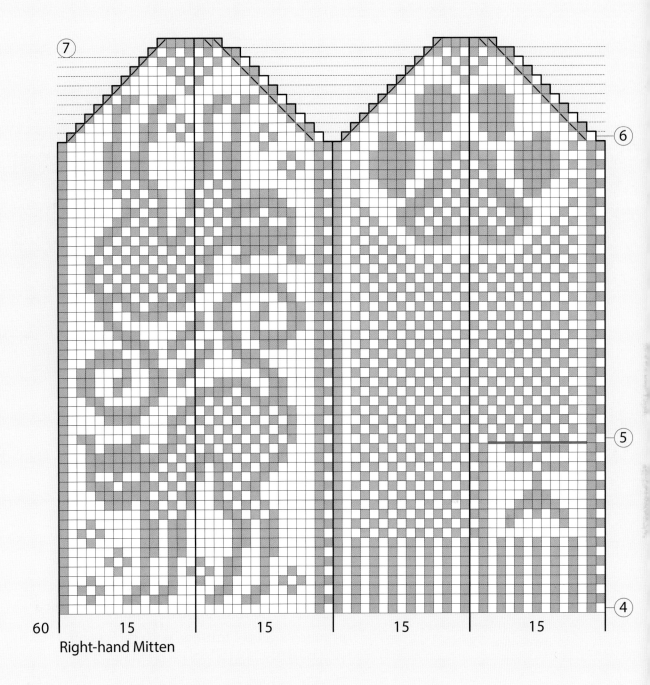

7

6

5

4

60

15   15   15   15

Right-hand Mitten

LITTLE RABBIT

MATERIALS

Small mittens
Yarn: CYCA #1 (sock/finger-ing/baby) Dale Garn Daletta (100% wool; 153 yd/140 m / 50 g), Light Blue #5703 and Natural White #0020
Needles: U.S. size 1.5 / 2.5 mm, set of 5 dpn

Large mittens
Yarn: CYCA #1 (sock/finger-ing/baby) Rauma Finullgarn (100% wool; 191 yd/175 m / 50 g), Rust Red #435 and White #400
Needles: U.S. size 2.5 / 3 mm, set of 5 dpn

Everyone falls for small, soft rabbits. Rabbits are a nice, cuddly animal to have and many children want to keep a little rabbit in a cage. It's not always possible to do that, of course—but everyone can have mittens with rabbits on them! These charming little rabbits are shown on both the front and back.

These mittens can be knitted in several sizes using the same charts (see the sizing guides on pages 13-17). For very small children, omit the thumb.

Instructions

With Light Blue (Rust Red), CO 44 sts. Divide the sts evenly onto 4 dpn (= 11 sts per ndl). Join, being careful not to twist cast-on row.

1) Begin with k1, p1 ribbing around. Use Chart A for small mittens without a thumb and Chart B for larger mittens with a thumb. Change colors as shown on charts.

2) After completing the ribbing, work following the chart for the right- and left-hand mittens (see page 32). On the first round, increase a total of 4 sts as shown on the chart = 48 sts.

3) You can substitute a name for the narrow 5-row pattern panel (see alphabet charts on page 214).

4) **Thumbhole:** The thick line on the chart indicates the placement of the thumbhole (blue line for left-hand mitten and red line for right). Knit the 9 sts for the thumb with smooth contrast color scrap yarn. Slide the sts back to the left needle and knit in pattern.

5) Continue following the chart up to the encircled 5, and then shape top by decreasing as shown on the chart.

6) When 5 sts each remain on the front and back, seam the sets of stitches with Kitchener stitch.

7) **Thumb:** Insert a dpn into the sts below the scrap yarn and another dpn into the sts above the scrap yarn. Remove the scrap yarn = 9 + 9 sts. On the first rnd of the thumb, increase to 22 sts total by picking up and knitting 2 sts at each side (see chart).

8) Work thumb to the encircled 8 and then shape top as shown on chart.

9) When 6 sts remain, cut yarn and draw end through rem sts. Weave in all yarn ends neatly on WS.

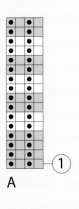

A

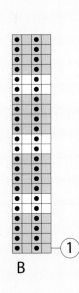

B

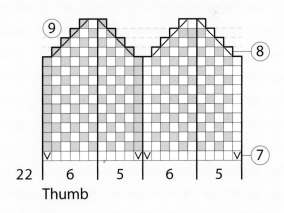

22 | 6 | 5 | 6 | 5

Thumb

		Knit
⊡	•	Purl
	Ⅴ	Increase 1 st
◪	☑	Right-leaning decrease
◩	◲	Left-leaning decrease

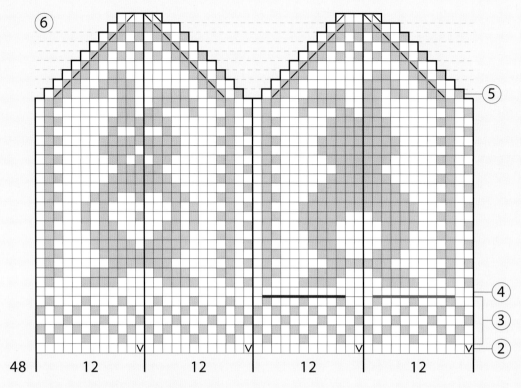

Right- and Left-hand Mittens

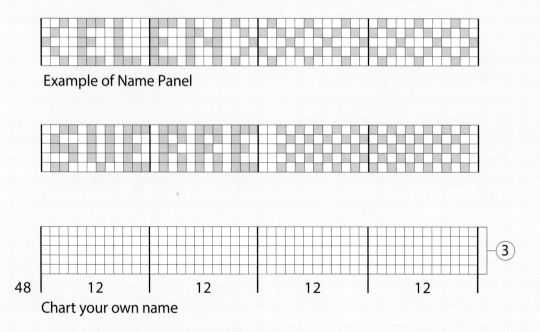

Example of Name Panel

Chart your own name

DOG MITTENS

MATERIALS
Yarn: CYCA #1 (sock/fingering/baby) Rauma Finullgarn (100% wool; 191 yd/175 m / 50 g), Black #436 and White #400
Needles: U.S. size 2.5 / 3 mm, set of 5 dpn

There is a wonderful website on the internet, a true knitting heaven, known as Ravelry.com. Millions of knitters from around the world meet on the forums there and show off what they've knitted, have discussions, buy and sell patterns and yarn, and offer wonderful inspiration for new projects. A Boston terrier named Bob is Ravelry's mascot, so these mittens with a picture of Bob were designed in honor of Ravelry.

Instructions

With Black, CO 56 sts. Divide the sts evenly onto 4 dpn (= 14 sts per ndl). Join, being careful not to twist cast-on row.

1) Begin by working the k1, p1 ribbing on the cuff chart below.

2) After completing the ribbing, on the chart row marked by the encircled 2, increase a total of 4 sts (one new st on each needle) = 60 sts.

3) After completing the cuff, continue, following the chart for the respective right- or left-hand mitten.

4) **Thumbhole:** The thick line on the chart indicates the placement of the thumbhole. Knit the 11 sts for the thumb with a smooth contrast color scrap yarn. Slide the sts back to the left needle and knit in pattern.

5) Continue following the chart up to the encircled 5, and then shape top by decreasing as shown on the chart.

6) When 7 sts each remain on the front and back, seam the sets of stitches with Kitchener stitch.

7) **Thumb:** Insert a dpn into the sts below the scrap yarn and another dpn into the sts above the scrap yarn. Remove the scrap yarn = 11 + 11 sts. On the first rnd of the thumb, increase to 26 sts total by picking up and knitting 2 sts at each side (see chart).

8) Work thumb to the encircled 8, and then shape top as shown on chart.

9) When 6 sts remain, cut yarn and draw end through rem sts. Weave in all yarn ends neatly on WS.

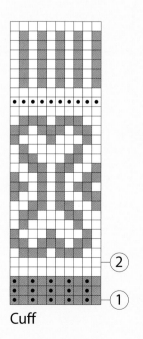

Cuff

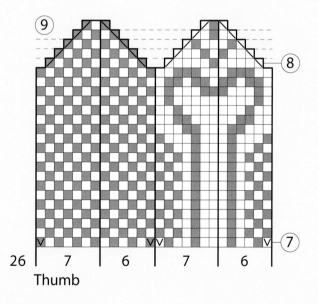

26   7   6   7   6

Thumb

		Knit
•	•	Purl
V	V	Increase 1 st
◪	◿	Right-leaning decrease
◩	◺	Left-leaning decrease

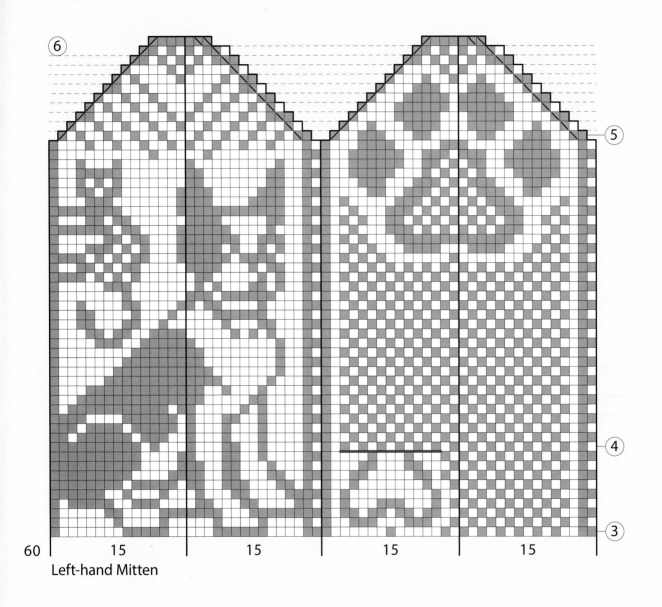

60

15　　　　15　　　　15　　　　15

Left-hand Mitten

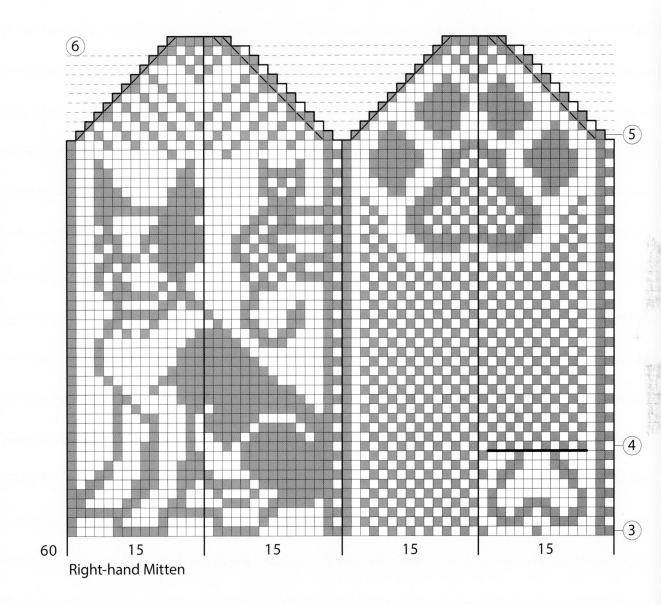

6

5

4

3

60   15   15   15   15

Right-hand Mitten

POODLE MITTENS

MATERIALS

Yarn: CYCA #1 (sock/ fingering/baby) Rauma Finullgarn (100% wool; 191 yd/175 m / 50 g), Natural White #401 and Brown #423

Needles: U.S. size 2.5 / 3 mm, set of 5 dpn

Many dog owners have contacted me to see if I would design a mitten pattern that accurately depicts their dog breed. No group has contacted me more than poodle owners, so I've designed this pattern especially for them. It's obvious that these showy dogs need their very own design!

Instructions

With Natural White, CO 56 sts. Divide the sts evenly onto 4 dpn (= 14 sts per ndl). Join, being careful not to twist cast-on row.

1) Begin by working the k1, p1 ribbing on the cuff chart below.

2) After completing the ribbing, on the chart row marked by the encircled 2, increase a total of 4 sts (one new st on each needle) = 60 sts.

3) After completing the cuff, continue, following the chart for the right- or left-hand mitten respectively.

4) **Thumbhole:** The thick line on the chart indicates the placement of the thumbhole. Knit the 11 sts for the thumb with a smooth contrast color scrap yarn. Slide the sts back to the left needle and knit in pattern.

5) Continue following the chart up to the encircled 5, and then shape top by decreasing as shown on the chart.

6) When 7 sts each remain on the front and back, seam the sets of stitches with Kitchener stitch.

7) **Thumb:** Insert a dpn into the sts below the scrap yarn and another dpn into the sts above the scrap yarn. Remove the scrap yarn = 11 + 11 sts. On the first rnd of the thumb, increase to 26 sts total by picking up and knitting 2 sts at each side (see chart).

8) Work thumb to the encircled 8, and then shape top as shown on chart.

9) When 6 sts remain, cut yarn and draw end through rem sts. Weave in all yarn ends neatly on WS.

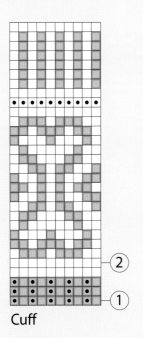

Cuff

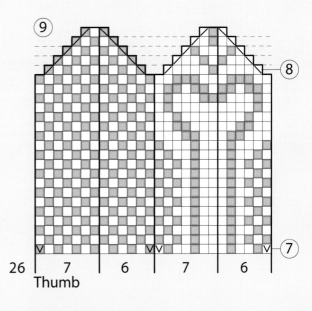

Thumb

		Knit
•	•	Purl
⩔	⩔	Increase 1 st
⧄	⧄	Right-leaning decrease
⧅	⧅	Left-leaning decrease

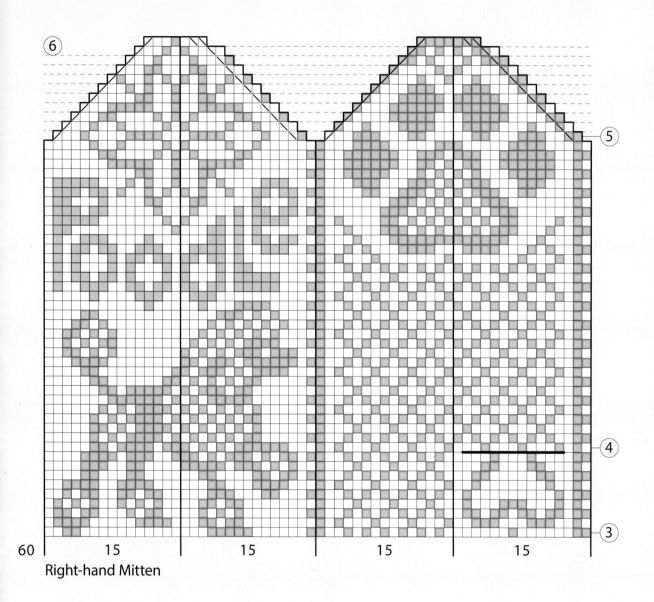

Right-hand Mitten

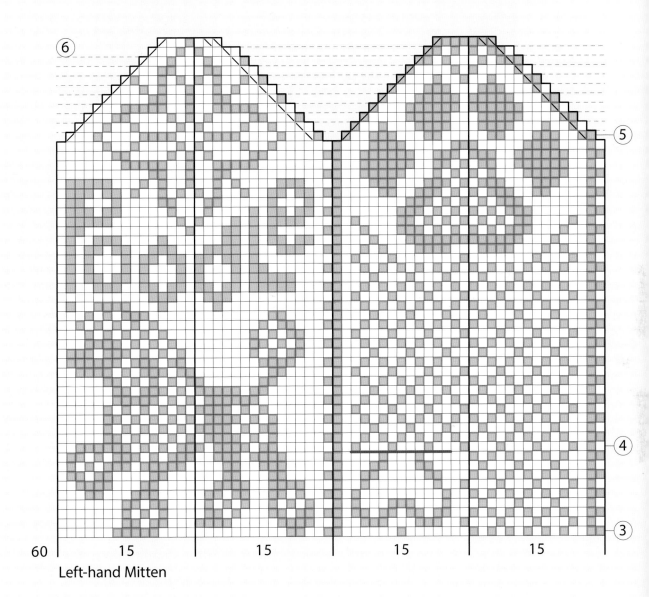

60 | 15 | 15 | 15 | 15 |

Left-hand Mitten

CAT AND MOUSE

MATERIALS
Yarn: CYCA #1 (sock/
fingering/baby) Sandnes
Garn Sisu (80% wool,
20% nylon; 191 yd/
175 m / 50 g), Purple
#5226, White #1001,
Turquoise #7024
Needles: U.S. size 1.5 /
2.5 mm, set of 5 dpn

The inspiration for this design is a girl
named Lotte. Lotte wanted some long mittens in her favorite colors, turquoise and
purple. She likes animals, cats and mice best
of all, so of course the mittens had to feature
them. Just to be safe, the cat and the mouse
are each on their own mitten. Snowflakes
surround them closely because Lotte loves it
when it snows!

The mittens will look extra nice with a
name panel, just in case the owner forgets
her mittens somewhere.

Instructions

With Purple, CO 60 sts. Divide the sts evenly onto 4 dpn (= 15 sts per ndl). Join, being careful not to twist cast-on row.

1) Begin by working the ribbing and narrow panels on the cuff chart below; the four-stitch motifs repeat around.

2) Chart and knit a name panel. Make sure the name is centered on the front of the mitten. If the name is longer than can be worked in 30 stitches, cut the white yarn and start the name panel on Ndl 3. In that case, the name will be centered between Ndls 2 and 3. After completing the panel, begin the round at the original point.

3) After completing the cuff, continue, following the chart for the right- or left-hand mitten respectively.

4) **Thumbhole:** The thick line on the chart indicates the placement of the thumbhole. Knit the 11 sts for the thumb with a smooth contrast color scrap yarn. Slide the sts back to the left needle and knit in pattern.

5) Continue following the chart up to the encircled 5, and then shape top by decreasing as shown on the chart.

6) When 7 sts each remain on the front and back, seam the sets of stitches with Kitchener stitch.

7) **Thumb:** Insert a dpn into the sts below the scrap yarn and another dpn into the sts above the scrap yarn. Remove the scrap yarn = 11 + 11 sts. On the first rnd of the thumb, increase to 26 sts total by picking up and knitting 2 sts at each side (see chart).

8) Work thumb in pattern as shown on chart row marked by an encircled 8. This pattern row is repeated 18 times.

9) At the encircled 9, shape top as shown on chart.

10) When 6 sts remain, cut yarn and draw end through rem sts. Weave in all yarn ends neatly on WS.

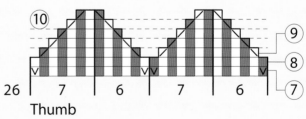

Thumb

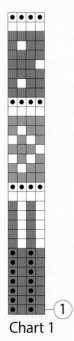

Chart 1

▨	▧	□	Knit
▪		⊡	Purl
	☑	☑	Increase 1 st
▧		╱	Right-leaning decrease
◣		╲	Left-leaning decrease

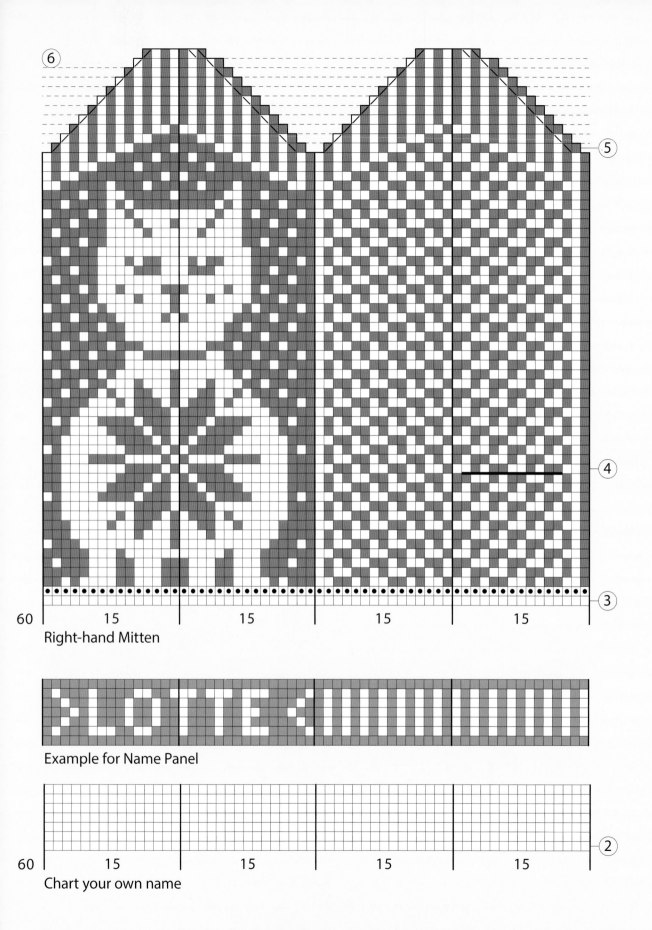

Right-hand Mitten

Example for Name Panel

Chart your own name

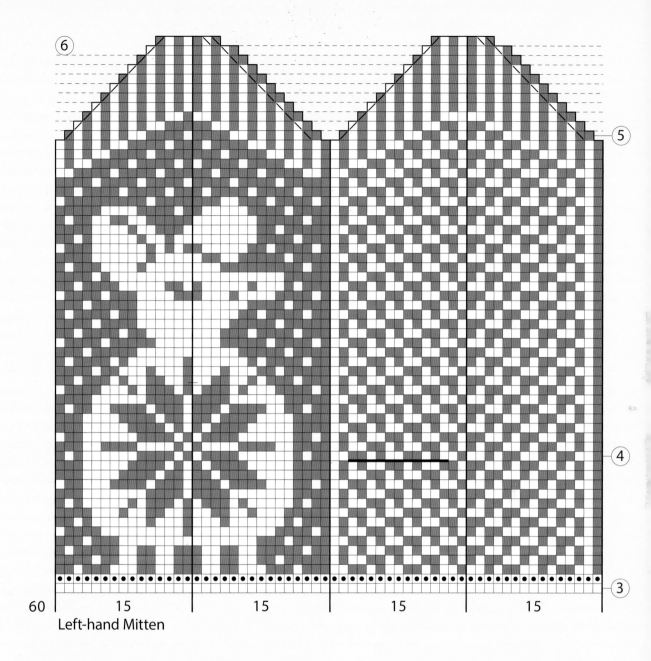

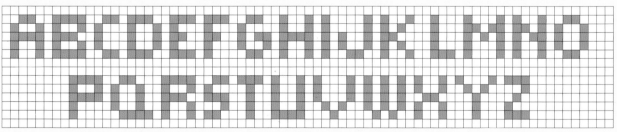

6

5

4

3

60   15   15   15   15

Left-hand Mitten

Alphabet for Name Panel

MITTENS WITH BIRD MOTIFS

You don't need to be an avowed bird lover to delight in the look of these fine creations.

Here is a selection of mittens with various birds as motifs. The birds have each been stylized for easy knitting.

BIRD MITTENS

MATERIALS
Yarn: CYCA #1 (sock/fingering/baby) Dale Garn Daletta (100% wool; 153 yd/140 m / 50 g), Light Blue #5703 and Black #0090 + small amount of Red #4018 for birds and hearts. A bird is embroidered with red on the palm of one mitten. The hearts on the back of each mitten's hand are embroidered with red.
Needles: U.S. size 2.5 / 3 mm, set of 5 dpn

These mittens were my very first design. The pattern was eventually published on my blog and I waited excitedly for the response.

After a while, I received an email from a Russian lady: "I have 3 children who are now adults and have flown from the nest, as the birds on the front of the mitten. My fourth child was adopted. She has Down's syndrome and will live with me as long as we both live. My good little girl is like the little bird in the hand, settled into my life after my other children became adults."

Instructions

With Light Blue (or lightest color), CO 58 sts. Divide the sts onto 4 dpn. Join, being careful not to twist cast-on row.

1) Work following the chart for the right- or left-hand mitten respectively.

2) **Thumbhole:** The thick line on the chart indicates the placement of the thumbhole. Knit the 11 sts for the thumb with a smooth contrast color scrap yarn. Slide the sts back to the left needle and knit in pattern.

3) Continue following the chart up to the encircled 3, and then shape top by decreasing as shown on the chart.

4) When 6 sts each remain on the front and back, seam the sets of stitches with Kitchener stitch.

5) **Thumb:** Insert a dpn into the sts below the scrap yarn and another dpn into the sts above the scrap yarn. Remove the scrap yarn = 11 + 11 sts. On the first rnd of the thumb, increase to 26 sts total by picking up and knitting 2 sts at each side (see chart).

6) At the encircled 6 on the thumb chart, decrease for the top as shown.

7) When 6 sts remain, cut yarn and draw end through rem sts. Weave in all yarn ends neatly on WS.

With Red and duplicate stitch, embroider the little bird on the palm of one mitten. On the back of the hand on both mittens, embroider a heart.

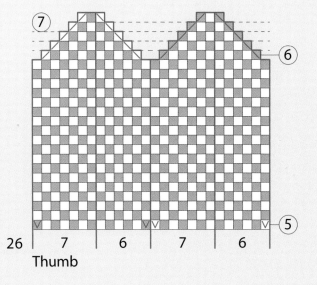

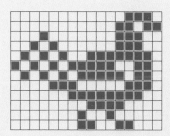

		Knit
	·	Purl
⊻	⊻	Increase 1 st
◿	◿	Right-leaning decrease
◺	◺	Left-leaning decrease

④

③

②

①

58 | 14 | 15 | 14 | 15

Right-hand Mitten

58   14   15   14   15

Left-hand Mitten

THE SOUTH POLE

MATERIALS

Yarn: CYCA #1 (sock/fingering/baby) Sandnes Garn Sisu (80% wool, 20% nylon; 191 yd/175 m / 50 g), Black #1099, Turquoise #7024, and White #1001

Needles: U.S. size 1.5 / 2.5 mm, set of 5 dpn

These mittens depict the summer landscape at the South Pole, with three happy penguins standing at the edge of the ice and warming themselves in the sunshine after a tasty fish dinner. The sea provides their source of food and life is good.

Instructions

Both mittens are knitted the same way except for the placement of the thumbhole and the directions the little penguins on the thumbs face.

With Black, CO 60 sts. Divide the sts evenly onto 4 dpn (= 15 sts per ndl). Join, being careful not to twist cast-on row. Work 5 rnds k2, p2 ribbing. Knit the next round, increasing to 64 sts *at the same time* (= K15, M1) 4 times—there should now be 16 sts on each dpn.

1) Begin by working the fish in Black and Turquoise from the chart below. The motif is repeated four times around.

2) At the chart row marked with an encircled 2, begin the ice floe. Hold the yarns so White is dominant and the ice will show well.

3) After completing the fish and ice chart, continue to the chart for the right- and left-hand mittens. Hold the yarns so Black is dominant on the palm.

4) **Thumbhole:** The thick line on the chart (blue line for left hand and red for right) indicates the placement of the thumbhole. Knit the 12 sts for the thumb with a smooth contrast color scrap yarn. Slide the sts back to the left needle and knit in pattern.

5) Continue following the chart up to the encircled 5 and then shape top by decreasing as shown on the chart.

6) When 8 sts each remain on the front and back, cut yarn and draw end through rem sts.

7) **Thumb:** Insert a dpn into the sts below the scrap yarn and another dpn into the sts above the scrap yarn. Remove the scrap yarn = 12 + 12 sts. On the first rnd of the thumb, increase to 28 sts total by picking up and knitting 2 sts at each side (see chart).

8) Making sure you work the correct thumb for each mitten, work thumb to chart row marked by encircled 8 and then shape top as shown.

9) When 8 sts remain, cut yarn and draw end through rem sts. Weave in all yarn ends neatly on WS.

▨	■ □	Knit
	⊡	Purl
	☑	Increase 1 st
◪	◿	Right-leaning decrease
◢	◺	Left-leaning decrease

Fish pattern

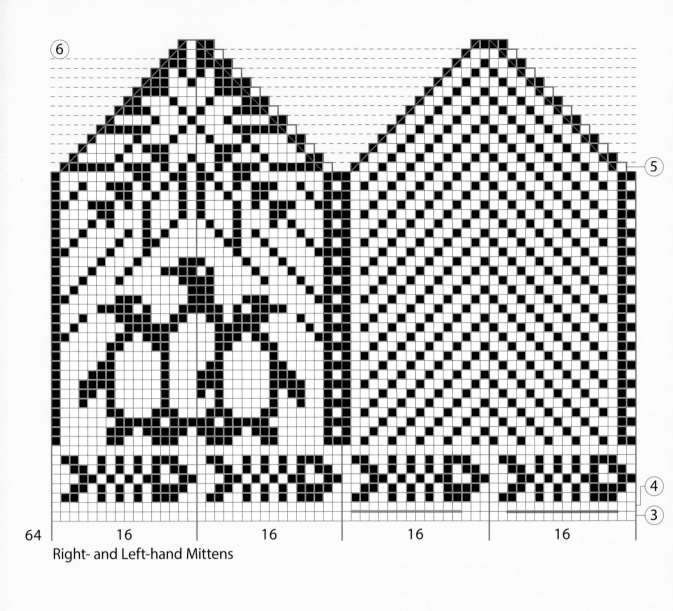

64 | 16 | 16 | 16 | 16

Right- and Left-hand Mittens

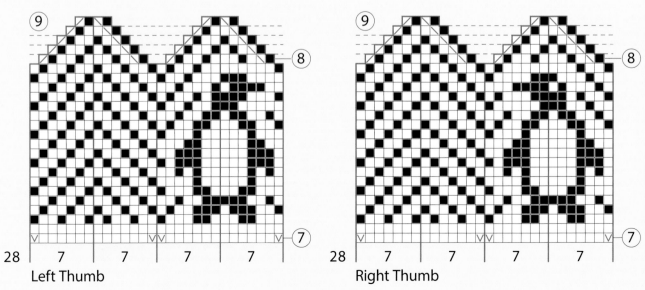

28 | 7 | 7 | 7 | 7

Left Thumb

28 | 7 | 7 | 7 | 7

Right Thumb

PTARMIGAN

MATERIALS
Yarn: CYCA #1 (sock/fingering/baby) Dale Garn Daletta (100% wool; 153 yd/140 m / 50 g), Dark Red #4255 and White #0010
Needles: U.S. size 2.5 / 3 mm, set of 5 dpn

Ptarmigans' feet do not freeze when they are cold. Their thick white coat of winter feathers goes right down to their toes. Ptarmigans are pretty birds beloved by many. You can find them all around Norway—and there are six of them right here on each mitten. They've left their footprints on the palm and thumbs. You can make longer or shorter mittens by simply adjusting the length of the ribbing.

Instructions

Both mittens are worked the same way except for the placement of the thumbhole.

With Red, CO 56 sts. Divide the sts onto 4 dpn = 14 sts on each needle. Join, being careful not to twist cast-on row.

For a short mitten, work 5 rnds of k1, p1 ribbing; for a longer mitten, work k2, p2 ribbing for 15 rnds.

1) Work following Chart 1. The motif is repeated 4 times around.

2) Now work following the chart for the right- and left-hand mittens. On the first rnd, increase 4 sts as indicated on the chart = 60 sts.

3) **Thumbhole:** The thick line on the chart indicates the placement of the thumbhole (blue line for the left hand and red for the right). Knit the 11 sts for the thumb with a smooth contrast color scrap yarn. Slide the sts back to the left needle and knit in pattern.

4) Continue following the chart to the encircled 4, and then shape top by decreasing as shown on the chart.

5) When 4 sts each remain on the front and back, cut yarn and draw end through rem sts.

6) **Thumb:** Insert a dpn into the sts below the scrap yarn and another dpn into the sts above the scrap yarn. Remove the scrap yarn = 11 + 11 sts. On the first rnd of the thumb, increase to 26 sts total by picking up and knitting 2 sts at each side (see chart).

7) Work to the encircled 7 on the thumb chart, and then shape top as shown.

8) When 6 sts remain, cut yarn and draw end through rem sts. Weave in all yarn ends neatly on WS.

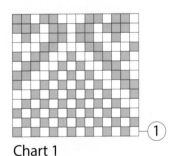

Chart 1

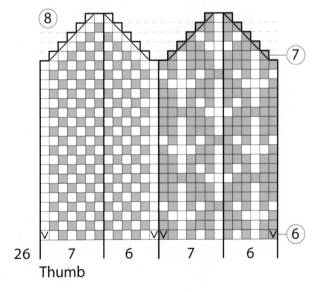

26 | 7 | 6 | 7 | 6

Thumb

▧	☐	Knit
☑	☑	Increase 1 st
◩	◪	Right-leaning decrease
◣	◺	Left-leaning decrease

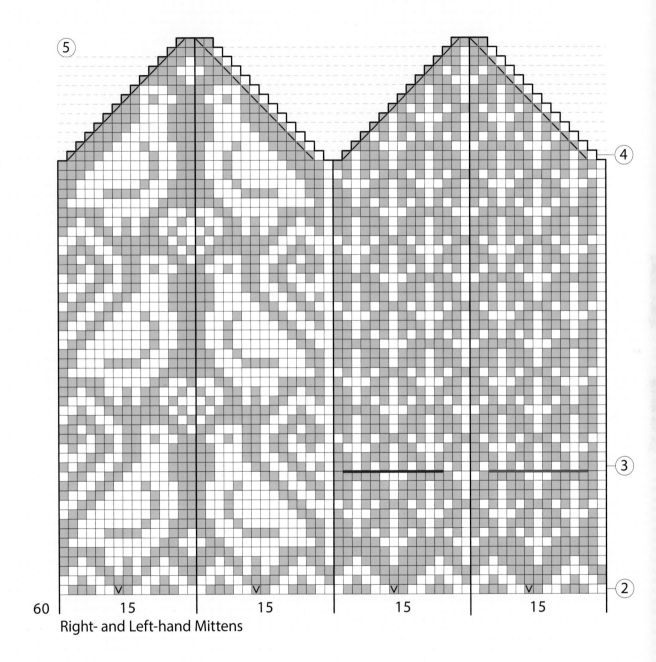

⑤

④

③

②

60 | 15   15   15   15

Right- and Left-hand Mittens

LITTLE BIRD

MATERIALS

Yarn: CYCA #3 (DK/ light worsted) Du Store Alpakka Sterk (40% Merino wool, 40% alpaca, 20% nylon; 150 yd/137 m / 50 g), Lilac #817 and White #806

Needles: U.S. size 2.5 / 3 mm, set of 5 dpn

These little birds are the same as those found on traditional bridal mittens—or maybe they're descended from the same birds? Our birds have their own little mittens to sit on. The hearts remind us that we shouldn't be afraid to devote ourselves to things that may one day fly away.

Instructions

With Lilac, CO 44 sts. Divide the sts onto 4 dpn = 11 sts per ndl. Join, being careful not to twist cast-on row.

1) Work following the ribbing chart below; k1, p1 is repeated around.

2) Next, work the chart for the right- or left-hand mitten respectively. As shown on the chart, increase 4 sts on the first round.

3) **Thumbhole:** The thick line on the chart indicates the placement of the thumbhole. Knit the 8 sts for the thumb with a smooth contrast color

scrap yarn. Slide the sts back to the left needle and knit in pattern.

4) From the point marked by an encircled 4, both mittens are worked alike.

5) Continue following the chart up to the encircled 5, and then shape top by decreasing as shown on the chart.

6) When 4 sts each remain on the front and back, cut yarn and draw end through rem sts.

7) **Thumb:** Insert a dpn into the sts below the scrap yarn and another

dpn into the sts above the scrap yarn. Remove the scrap yarn = 8 + 8 sts. On the first rnd of the thumb, increase to 18 sts total by picking up and knitting 1 st at each side (see chart). Work chart 2 times on each round—the back and front of thumb are alike.

8) At the encircled 8 on the thumb chart, decrease for the top as shown.

9) When 6 sts remain, cut yarn and draw end through rem sts. Weave in all yarn ends neatly on WS.

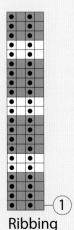

Ribbing

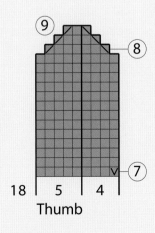

18 5 4

Thumb

  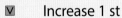

■ ☐　Knit
● ⊡　Purl
☑　　Increase 1 st
◩ ☑　Right-leaning decrease
◪ ◩　Left-leaning decrease

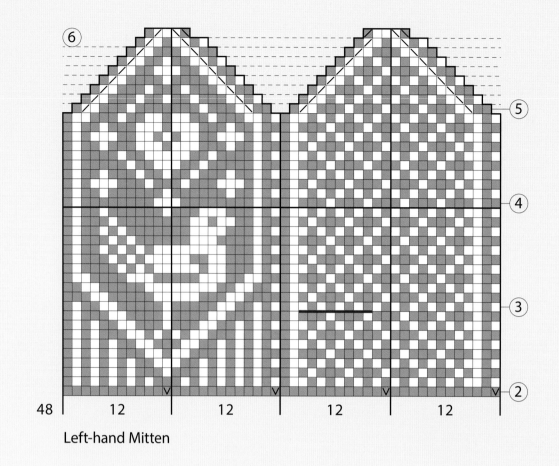

Left-hand Mitten

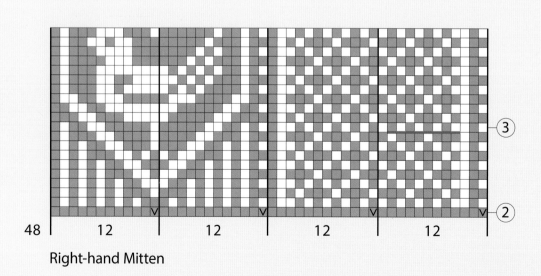

Right-hand Mitten

NIGHT OWL

MATERIALS

Yarn: CYCA #1 (sock/fingering/baby) Sandnes Garn Sisu (80% wool, 20% nylon; 191 yd/175 m / 50 g), Charcoal #1088 and Light Gray Heather #1032

Needles: U.S. size 1.5 / 2.5 mm, set of 5 dpn

Are you the type who stays up knitting into the wee hours, thinking, "Just one more row—just to see how it will look"? Do you keep repeating that thought one row after another? And then before you know it, the sun is rising! The night owl is a pretty design, and easy to knit. When the hand of the mitten is finished, there's another little baby owl on the thumb.

Instructions

With Charcoal (darkest color), CO 60 sts. Divide the sts evenly onto 4 dpn (= 15 sts per ndl). Join, being careful not to twist cast-on row.

1) Begin by working the ribbing from the chart below (k2, p2) around. If you want a more snugly fitted cuff, work the ribbing with a needle one size smaller than for the rest of the mitten.

2) After completing the ribbing, continue, following the chart for the right- or left-hand mitten respectively.

3) **Thumb gusset:** Increase 2 sts on every other round as indicated on the chart. After completing all thumb gusset increases, there should be 68 sts total.

4) **Thumbhole:** The thick line on the chart (blue line for left hand and red for right) indicates the placement of the thumb-hole. Knit the 13 sts for the thumb with a smooth contrast color scrap yarn. Slide the sts back to the left needle and knit in pattern.
Right-hand mitten: After completing chart, continue as for the left-hand mitten above the fine red line.

5) Continue following the chart up to the encircled 5, and then shape top by decreasing as shown on the chart.

6) When 9 sts each remain on the front and back, seam the sets of sts with Kitchener st.

7) **Thumb:** Insert a dpn into the sts below the scrap yarn and another dpn into the sts above the scrap yarn. Remove the scrap yarn = 13 + 13 sts. On the first rnd of the thumb, increase to 30 sts total by picking up and knitting 2 sts at each side (see chart).

8) When you reach the row marked with an encircled 8, shape top as shown on chart.

9) When 6 sts remain, cut yarn and draw end through rem sts. Weave in all yarn ends neatly on WS.

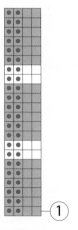

Knit

		Ribbing
		Purl
		Increase 1 st
		Right-leaning decrease
		Left-leaning decrease

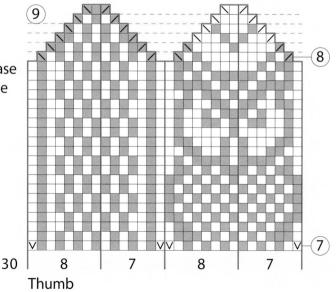

30 | 8 | 7 | 8 | 7

Thumb

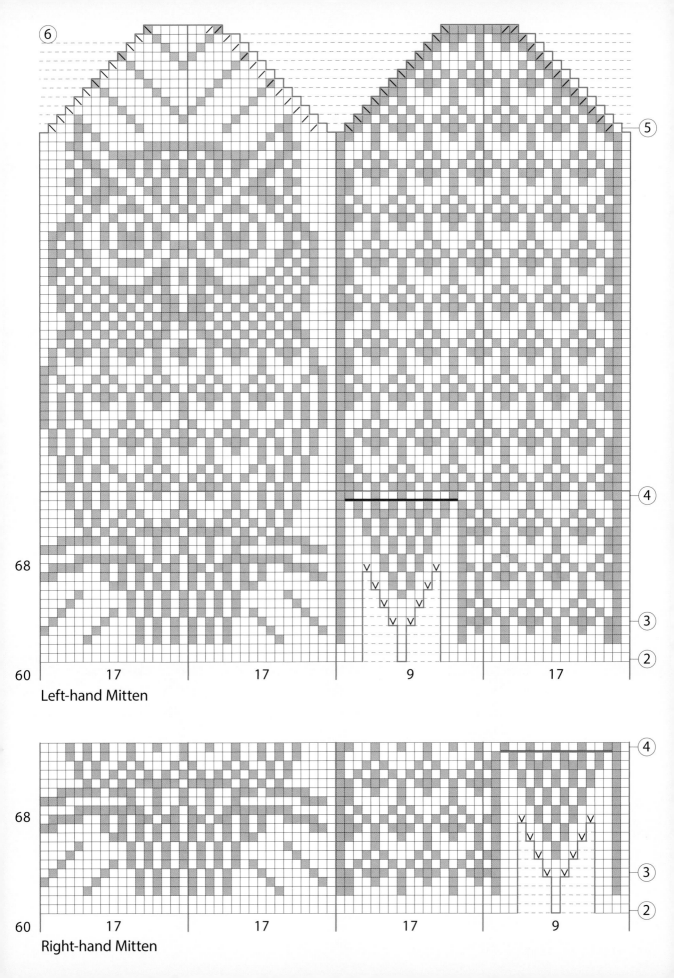

Left-hand Mitten

Right-hand Mitten

FELTED MITTENS

Nothing is warmer or feels better than felted mittens! These mittens are knitted on large needles and then felted to size in the washing machine.

With few stitches around and motifs that are easy to knit, these mittens will be finished in a flash.

It can be a bit tricky to get the sizing right on felted mittens. A number of factors come into play: yarn, needle size, gauge—and, of course, your washing machine!

Use a yarn that is recommended for felting—pure new wool, not superwash. Tove from Sandnes Garn is a nice yarn that is especially good for felting.

The mittens are knitted on needles that are U.S. size 6 or 7 / 4 or 4.5 mm.

How to felt

Before you felt the mittens, weave in all the yarn ends. Mittens can be felted with mild dishwashing soap or wool wash. Put the mittens into the washer with a hand towel and the soap. Wash at 86°F / 30°C on the normal program (do not use the gentle cycle for woolens). If you are felting several items *at the same time*, you can omit the towel. The fuller the machine is, the more the garments will felt. After completing the felting, pat the mittens out to correct measurements and leave flat until dry. To make the mittens extra soft and fluffy, brush the surface after the mittens are dry.

BURNING LOVE

MATERIALS
Yarn:
Smaller size mittens (see photos on pages 18 and 65):
CYCA #3 (DK/light worsted) Gjestal Østlandsgarn (Gjestal Vestlandsgarn or Dale of Norway Heilo can substitute) (100% wool; 109 yd/100 m / 50 g), Natural White, Yellow, and Dark Red
Needles: U.S. size 7 / 4.5 mm

Larger size mittens:
CYCA #2 (sport/baby) Sandnes Garn Tove (100% wool; 175 yd/160 m / 50 g), Natural White #1012, Orange #3326, Dark Red #4228
Needles: U.S. size 7 / 4.5 mm, set of 5 dpn

Just seeing these mittens will warm you. Love burns with intense flames. The design will also be pretty in cooler colors. You can experiment with all sorts of combinations!

Instructions

Both mittens are knitted the same way except for the placement of the thumb.

With Natural White, CO 48 sts. Knit 4 rows of garter st back and forth = 2 garter ridges. Now divide the sts onto 4 dpn = 12 sts per ndl. Join, being careful not to twist.

1) Work following the chart on page 68; the pattern is worked two times—both sides of the mitten are identical. Of course, only one thumb is worked on each mitten.

2) At the chart row marked with an encircled 2, work 9 rnds k2, p2 ribbing.

3) **Thumbhole:** The thick line on the chart indicates the placement of the thumbhole (blue line for left mitten; red for right). Knit the 9 sts for the thumb with a smooth contrast color scrap yarn. Slide the sts back to the left needle and knit in pattern.

4) Continue following the chart up to the encircled 4, and then shape top by decreasing as shown on the chart.

5) When 4 sts each remain on the front and back, cut yarn and draw end through rem sts.

6) **Thumb:** Insert a dpn into the sts below the scrap yarn and another dpn into the sts above the scrap yarn. Remove the scrap yarn = 9 + 9 sts. On the first rnd of the thumb, increase to 20 sts total by picking up and knitting 1 st at each side (see chart).

7) At the encircled 7 on the thumb chart, decrease for the top as shown.

8) When 4 sts remain, cut yarn and draw end through rem sts. Seam the garter stitch band at lower edge of each mitten cuff. Weave in all yarn ends neatly on WS.

Felt mittens following instructions on page 64.

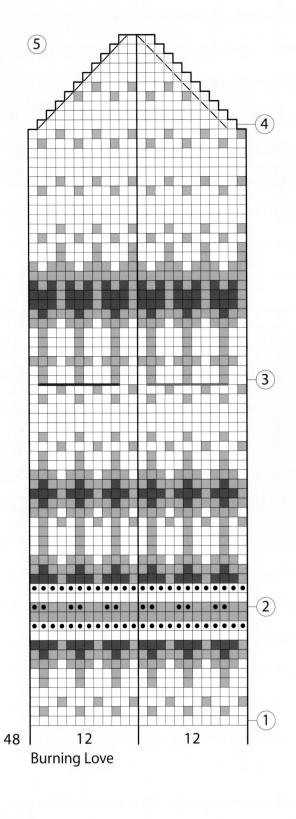

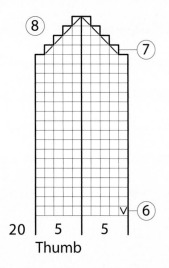

Knit

Purl

Increase 1 st

Right-leaning decrease

Left-leaning decrease

⑤

④

③

②

①

48

12

12

Burning Love

⑧

⑦

⑥

20

5

5

Thumb

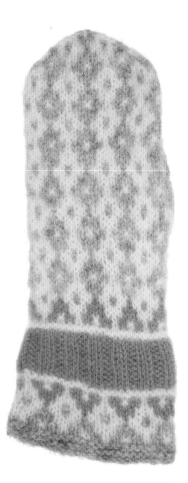

DIAMOND COOKIES

MATERIALS

These mittens were loosely knitted with Tove. This pair has been well used for an entire winter and washed several times with mild soap. They've retained their softness and warmth. A few pills have come to the surface; if your mittens pill, just pick the pills off.

Yarn: CYCA #2 (sport/baby) Sandnes Garn Tove (100% wool; 175 yd/160 m / 50 g), Gray #1053, Light Gray #1035, Mauve #4342
Needles: U.S. size 7 / 4.5 mm, set of 5 dpn

At Christmas, we bake diamond cookies (we call them sirupssnipper) and top each with an almond half in the center. These mittens are covered with Christmas diamond cookies. Mauve is one of the colors associated with Christmas here, and so these mittens have a mauve panel in honor of this lovely season.

Instructions

Both mittens are knitted the same way except for the placement of the thumb. The half almond is worked with a knit and purl, with the purl over the knit on the following round.

With Dark Gray, CO 48 sts. Knit 4 rows of garter st back and forth = 2 garter ridges. Now divide the sts onto 4 dpn = 12 sts per ndl. Join, being careful not to twist.

1) Work following the chart on page 72; the pattern is worked two times and both sides of the mitten are identical. Of course, only one thumb is worked on each mitten.

2) At the chart row marked with an encircled 2, work 9 rnds k2, p2 ribbing.

3) **Thumbhole:** The thick line on the chart indicates the placement of the thumbhole (blue line for left mitten; red for right). Knit the 9 sts for the thumb with a smooth contrast color scrap yarn. Slide the sts back to the left needle and knit in pattern.

4) Continue following the chart up to the encircled 4 and then shape top by decreasing as shown on the chart.

5) When 4 sts each remain on the front and back, cut yarn and draw end through rem sts.

6) **Thumb:** Insert a dpn into the sts below the scrap yarn and another dpn into the sts above the scrap yarn. Remove the scrap yarn = 9 + 9 sts. On the first rnd of the thumb, increase to 20 sts total by picking up and knitting 1 st at each side (see chart).

7) At the encircled 7 on the thumb chart, decrease for the top as shown.

8) When 4 sts remain, cut yarn and draw end through rem sts. Seam the garter stitch band at lower edge of each mitten cuff. Weave in all yarn ends neatly on WS.

Felt mittens following instructions on page 64.

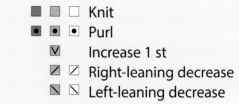

Knit
Purl
Increase 1 st
Right-leaning decrease
Left-leaning decrease

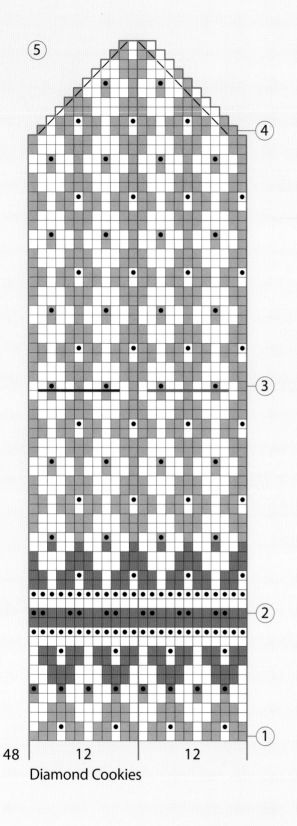

⑤

④

③

②

①

48 | 12 | 12

Diamond Cookies

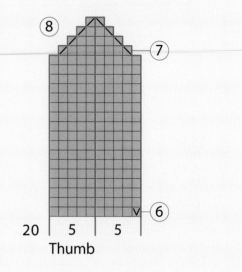

⑧

⑦

⑥

20 | 5 | 5

Thumb

FLY AGARIC MUSHROOMS

MATERIALS

These mittens were loosely knitted with Tove. The mittens were felted in the washing machine in one cycle at 86°F / 30°C, with mild dish soap.

Yarn: CYCA #2 (sport/baby) Sandnes Garn Tove (100% wool; 175 yd/160 m / 50 g), Red #4120 and White #1012

Needles: U.S. size 7 / 4.5 mm, set of 5 dpn

Fly agaric mushrooms are poisonous—but beautiful! With few stitches around and a pattern motif that practically knits itself, these mittens will be a fast project. And they'll come out just as well in a color other than red—why not blue fly agaric? The spots stand out a little from the background because they're worked with two white stitches, as a knit stitch on one round and a purl on the next round.

Instructions

Both mittens are knitted the same way except for the placement of the thumb.

With White, CO 48 sts. Knit 4 rows of garter st back and forth = 2 garter ridges. Now divide the sts onto 4 dpn = 12 sts per ndl. Join, being careful not to twist.

1) Work following the chart on page 75; the pattern is worked two times and both sides of the mitten are identical. Of course, only one thumb is worked on each mitten.

2) At the chart row marked with an encircled 2, work 9 rnds k2, p2 ribbing.

3) **Thumbhole:** The thick line on the chart indicates the placement of the thumbhole (blue line for left mitten; black for right). Knit the 9 sts for the thumb with a smooth contrast color scrap yarn. Slide the sts back to the left needle and knit in pattern.

4) Continue following the chart up to the encircled 4, and then shape top by decreasing as shown on the chart.

5) When 4 sts each remain on the front and back, cut yarn and draw end through rem sts.

6) **Thumb:** Insert a dpn into the sts below the scrap yarn and another dpn into the sts above the scrap yarn. Remove the scrap yarn = 9 + 9 sts. On the first rnd of the thumb, increase to 20 sts total by picking up and knitting 1 st at each side (see chart).

7) At the encircled 7 on the thumb chart, decrease for the top as shown.

8) When 4 sts remain, cut yarn and draw end through rem sts. Seam the garter stitch band at lower edge of each mitten cuff. Weave in all yarn ends neatly on WS.

Felt mittens following instructions on page 64.

Knit, Purl, Increase, and Decrease Legend

- ☐ Knit
- ● ⊡ Purl
- ☑ Increase 1 st
- ◩ ◹ Right-leaning decrease
- ◪ ◺ Left-leaning decrease

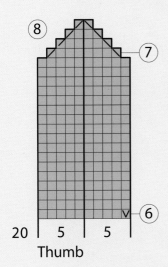

⑧ ⑦ ⑥

20 | 5 | 5

Thumb

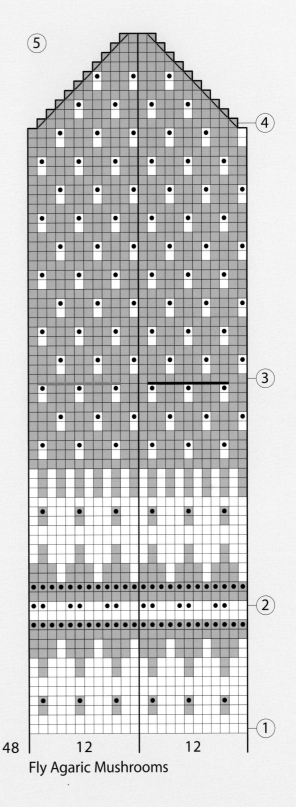

⑤ ④ ③ ② ①

48 | 12 | 12

Fly Agaric Mushrooms

WHITE TIGER

MATERIALS

These mittens were loosely knitted with Tove. The mittens in the photo were felted a little too vigorously in the washing machine so the tiger stripes are not as clear as intended.

Yarn: CYCA #2 (sport/baby) Sandnes Garn Tove (100% wool; 175 yd/160 m / 50 g), White #1012 and Charcoal #1088

Needles: U.S. size 7 / 4.5 mm, set of 5 dpn

The stripe patterns in the tiger's fur help it blend in with the shadows of the jungle. A tiger can be difficult to spot unless you're keeping an eye out for it. You might also need to look twice at the mittens before the striping becomes obvious. After they've been felted, these mittens will look just like a tiger's fur.

Instructions

Both mittens are knitted the same way except for the placement of the thumb.

With White, CO 48 sts. Divide the sts onto 4 dpn = 12 sts per ndl and join, being careful not to twist. Work 4 rnds in k2, p2 ribbing.

1) Work following the chart on page 78; use same chart for right- and left-hand mittens. On Rnd 1, increase to 50 sts as indicated on the chart.

2) At the chart row marked with an encircled 2, decrease 2 sts as shown on chart.

3) At the chart row marked with an encircled 3, work k2, p2 around. Repeat this round 6 times.

4) At the chart row marked with an encircled 4, increase 2 sts as shown on chart.

5) **Thumbhole:** The thick line on the chart indicates the placement of the respective left and right thumbholes. Knit the 9 sts for the thumb with a smooth contrast color scrap yarn. Slide the sts back to the left needle and knit in pattern.

6) Continue following the chart up to the encircled 6, and then shape top by decreasing as shown on the chart.

7) When 5 sts each remain on the front and back, cut yarn and draw end through rem sts.

8) **Thumb:** Insert a dpn into the sts below the scrap yarn and another dpn into the sts above the scrap yarn. Remove the scrap yarn = 9 + 9 sts. On the first rnd of the thumb, increase to 22 sts total by picking up and knitting 2 sts at each side (see chart).

9) At the encircled 9 on the thumb chart, decrease for the top as shown.

10) When 6 sts remain, cut yarn and draw end through rem sts. Weave in all yarn ends neatly on WS.

Felt mittens following instructions on page 64.

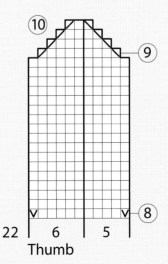

22 | 6 | 5

Thumb

	Knit
⊡	Purl
V	Increase 1 st
⧄	Right-leaning decrease
⧅	Left-leaning decrease

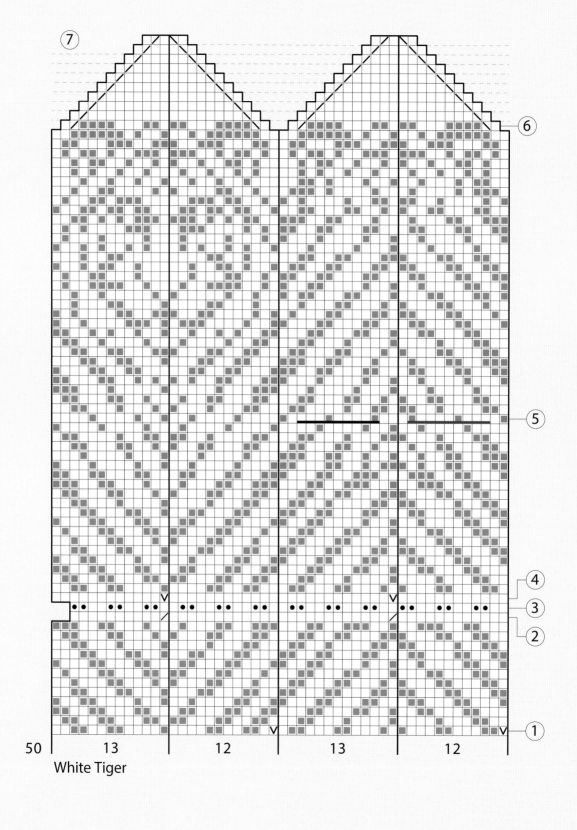

50

13   12   13   12

White Tiger

MITTENS WITH SYMBOLS

These patterns have symbolic motifs that one must examine closely to discern the shapes. Well-known symbols, colors, and lines are delicately interwoven so that they both follow and emphasize the fine shape of the hand.

JORID'S CHRISTMAS HEARTS

MATERIALS

Yarn:

Dark Mittens: CYCA #1 (sock/fingering/baby) Rauma Finullgarn (100% wool; 191 yd/175 m / 50 g), White #400, Dark Red #435, Deep Turquoise #438

Needles: U.S. size 2.5 / 3 mm, set of 5 dpn

Light Mittens: CYCA #4 (worsted/afghan/aran) Trysil Garn Alpa (65% acrylic, 20% alpaca, 15% wool; 153 yd/140 m / 50 g), White, Old Rose, Purple

Needles: U.S. size 2.5 / 3 mm

Right before Christmas is a good time of year. After the stress of the day, you can lean back in your chair and get cozy with a cup of tea and your knitting. It's so nice to make your Christmas gifts in such a comfortable way. Don't forget to knit love and good Christmas wishes into each stitch!

These Christmas heart mittens are easy to knit because the pattern can be memorized quickly.

Instructions

Both mittens are worked the same way except for the placement of the thumb.

With Purple (Deep Turquoise), CO 56 sts. Divide the sts evenly onto 4 dpn (= 14 sts per ndl). Join, being careful not to twist cast-on row.

1) Begin by working the ribbing on the cuff chart below.

2) After completing the cuff chart, continue, following the chart for left- and right-hand mittens. On Rnd 1 (marked by the encircled 2), increase a total of 4 sts (one new st on each needle) = 60 sts.

3) On the chart row marked by the encircled 3, increase 1 st at the side. This stitch will always be purled and will make the transition between rounds smoother. It won't be visible in the finished mitten.

4) **Thumbhole:** The thick line on the chart (black line for left-hand thumb and red for right) indicates the placement of the thumbhole. Knit the 11 sts for the thumb with a smooth contrast color scrap yarn. Slide the sts back to the left needle and knit in pattern.

5) Continue following the chart up to the encircled 5, and then decrease 1 st (the purl st).

6) Shape top by decreasing as shown on the chart.

7) When 7 sts each remain on the front and back, seam the sets of stitches with Kitchener stitch.

8) **Thumb:** Insert a dpn into the sts below the scrap yarn and another dpn into the sts above the scrap yarn. Remove the scrap yarn = 11 + 11 sts. On the first rnd of the thumb, increase to 26 sts total by picking up and knitting 2 sts at each side (see chart).

9) Work thumb to encircled 9 and then shape top as shown on chart.

10) When 6 sts remain, cut yarn and draw end through rem sts. Weave in all yarn ends neatly on WS.

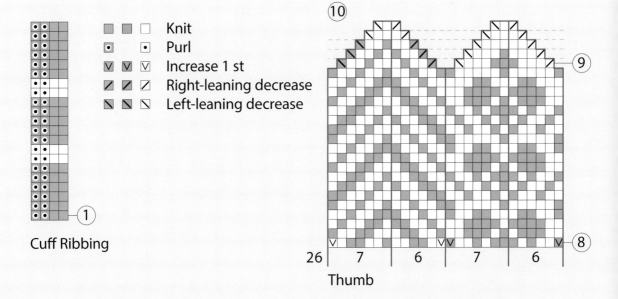

	Knit
	Purl
	Increase 1 st
	Right-leaning decrease
	Left-leaning decrease

Cuff Ribbing

Thumb

26 | 7 | 6 | 7 | 6

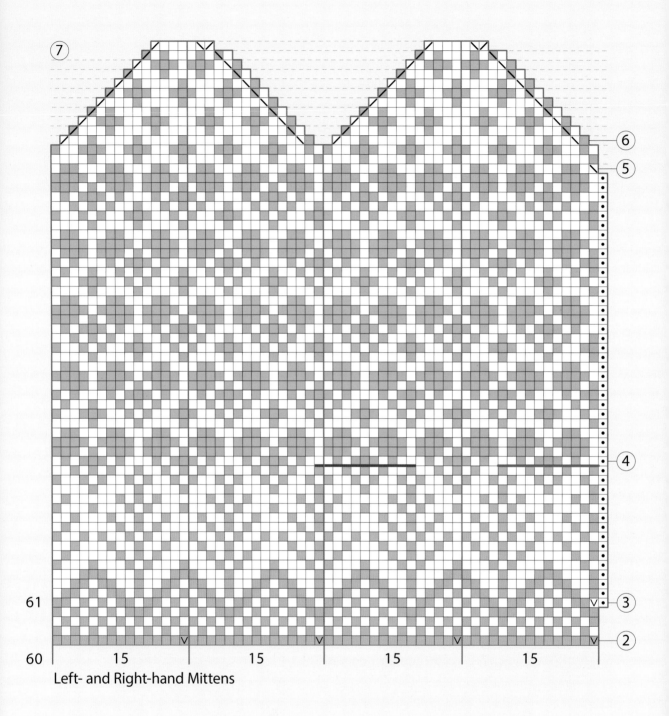

Left- and Right-hand Mittens

ICE CRYSTAL

MATERIALS

Yarn:

Multi-color: CYCA #1 (sock/finger-ing/baby) Garnstudio (Drops) Fabel Print (75% wool, 25% nylon; 224 yd/205 m / 50 g), Blue Lagoon #340 This yarn has the same fine blue shades as the sky itself.

White: CYCA #1 (sock/fingering/baby) Sandnes Garn Sisu (80% wool, 20% nylon; 191 yd/175 m / 50 g), Charcoal #1088, Light Gray Heather #1032

Needles: U.S. size 1.5 / 2.5 mm, set of 5 dpn

Sometimes on winter days all the windows in the kids' rooms are covered with ice crystals—carefully cut out of paper. These white patterns stand out so prettily against the background of the blue winter sky, and thus the idea for these ice crystal mittens was born. The pattern on these lovely mittens emphasizes the elegant curve of the wrist.

Instructions

With White, CO 60 sts. Divide the sts evenly onto 4 dpn (= 15 sts per ndl). Join, being careful not to twist cast-on row.

1) Begin by working the chart for the left- or right-hand mitten respectively. **NOTE:** Work Rnd 1 of k1, p1 ribbing for a total of 11 rounds.

2) At the chart row marked with the encircled 2, repeat the row for a total of 12 rounds. After completing the 12 rnds, continue following the chart, working each row only once.

3) Thumb gusset: Increase 2 sts on every other round as indicated on the chart. After completing all thumb gusset increases, there should be 68 sts total.

4) **Thumbhole:** The thick line on the chart indicates the placement of the thumbhole. Knit the 13 sts for the thumb with a smooth contrast color scrap yarn. Slide the sts back to the left needle and knit in pattern. Right-hand mitten: After completing chart through thumbhole, continue as for the left-hand mitten above the fine red line.

5) Continue following the chart up to the encircled 5, and then shape top by decreasing as shown on the chart.

6) When 9 sts each remain on the front and back, seam the sets of sts with Kitchener st.

7) **Thumb:** Insert a dpn into the sts below the scrap yarn and another dpn into the sts above the scrap yarn. Remove the scrap yarn = 13 + 13 sts. On the first rnd of the thumb, increase to 30 sts total by picking up and knitting 2 sts at each side (see chart).

8) When you reach the row marked with an encircled 8, shape top as shown on chart.

9) When 6 sts remain, cut yarn and draw end through rem sts. Weave in all yarn ends neatly on WS.

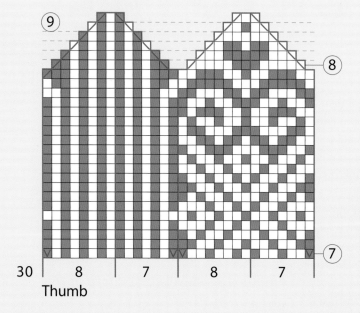

30 | 8 | 7 | 8 | 7

Thumb

☐ Knit
☐ Purl
☑ Increase 1 st
☑ Right-leaning decrease
☐ Left-leaning decrease

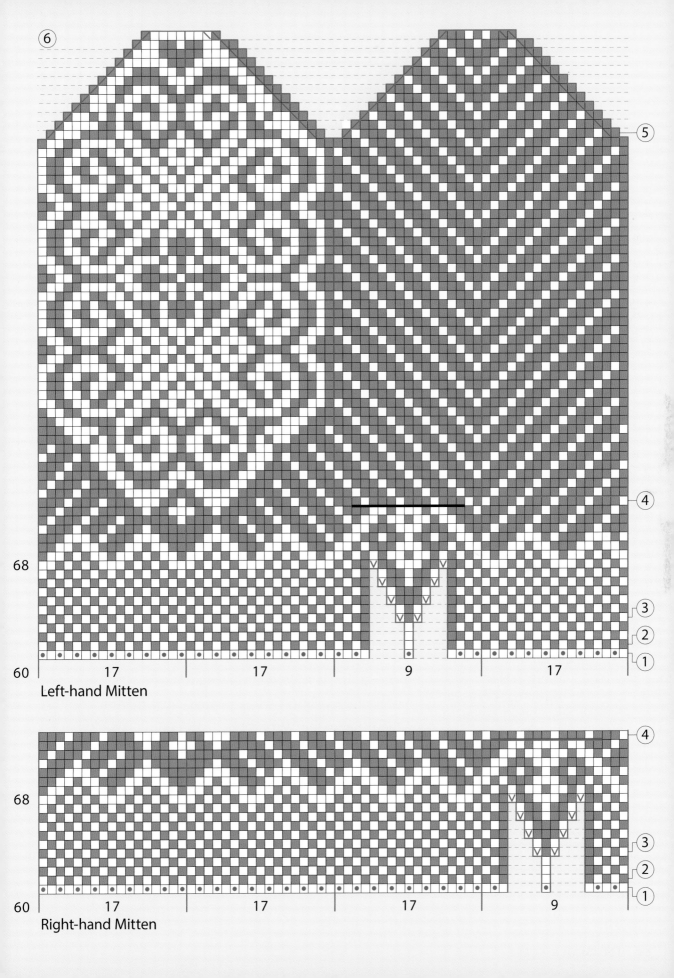

Left-hand Mitten

Right-hand Mitten

TALLULAH'S HEART

MATERIALS

Yarn: CYCA #1 (sock/fingering/baby) Dale Garn Daletta (100% wool; 153 yd/140 m / 50 g), Black #0090 and Dark Red #4255

Needles: U.S. size 1.5 / 2.5 mm, set of 5 dpn

"Tallulah" is a Native American name of uncertain origin—some people say it means "leaping water." When I hear the name, I know I can almost see water swirling in a beck. The motif and the color choice were inspired by Norwegian folk painting tradition. The painted swirls often create fine heart shapes, which you'll see if you look closely.

Instructions

With Black, CO 54 sts. Divide the sts onto 4 dpn. Join, being careful not to twist cast-on row. Work 18 rnds of the cuff pattern: (K2 with Dark Red, p1 with Black) around.

1) After completing the ribbing, work following the chart for the right- or left-hand mitten respectively (see page 90). On the first round, increase 2 sts as shown on the chart.

2) **Thumb Gusset:** Increase 2 sts on every other round as shown on the chart. When all the increases have been made, there should be a total of 68 sts around.

3) **Thumbhole:** The thick line on the chart indicates the placement of the thumbhole. Knit the 12 sts for the thumb with a smooth contrast color scrap yarn. Slide the sts back to the left needle and knit in pattern. At the chart row with an en-circled 3, continue the left and right mittens from the same chart.

4) Continue following the chart up to the encircled 4, and then shape top by decreasing as shown on the chart.

5) When 10 sts each remain on the front and back, seam the sets of stitches with Kitchener stitch.

6) **Thumb:** Insert a dpn into the sts below the scrap yarn and another dpn into the sts above the scrap yarn. Remove the scrap yarn = 12 + 12 sts. On the first rnd of the thumb, increase to 28 sts total by picking up and knitting 2 sts at each side (see chart).

7) Work thumb to en-circled 7 and then shape top as shown on chart.

8) When 8 sts remain, cut yarn and draw end through rem sts. Weave in all yarn ends neatly on WS.

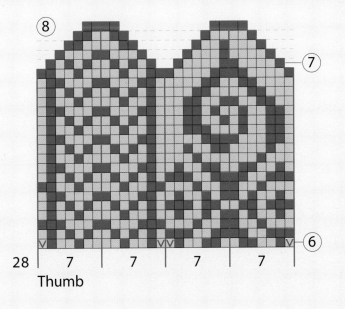

		Knit
	☑	Increase 1 st
	◩	Right-leaning decrease
	◪	Left-leaning decrease

28   7   7   7   7

Thumb

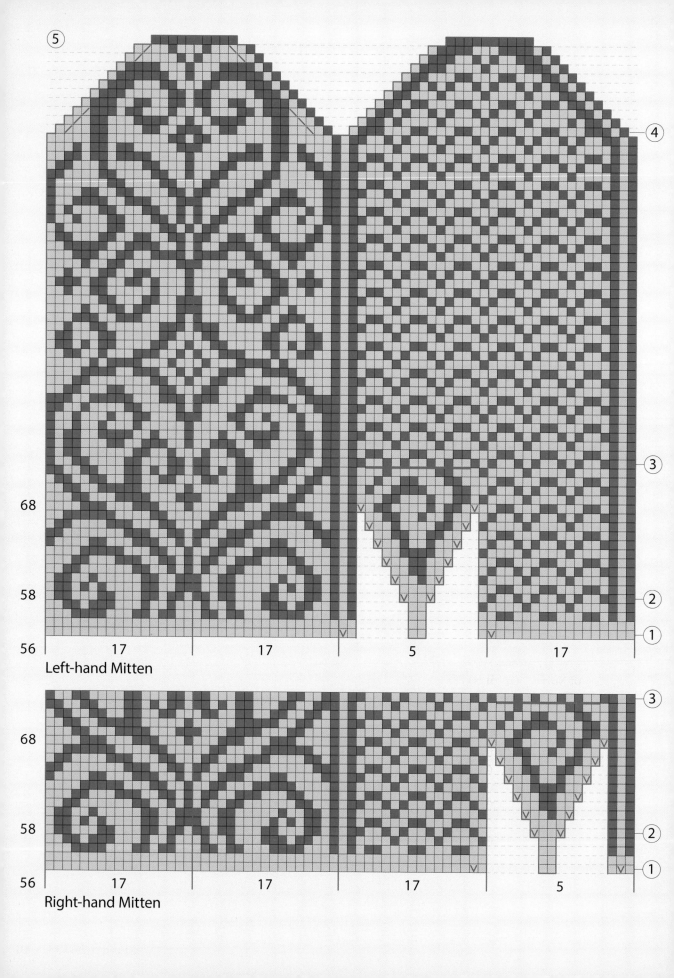

⑤

④

③

68

58

56   17   17   5   17

② ①

Left-hand Mitten

③

68

58

56   17   17   17   5

② ①

Right-hand Mitten

FLYING HEARTS

MATERIALS

Yarn: CYCA #1 (sock/fingering/baby) Viking of Norway Nordlys (75% wool, 25% nylon; 382 yd/349 m / 100 g), Red-Purple-Blue-Yellow #949; CYCA #1 (sock/fingering/baby) Sandnes Garn Sisu (80% wool, 20% nylon; 191 yd/175 m / 50 g), Black #1099

Needles: U.S. size 2.5 / 3 mm, set of 5 dpn

Winged hearts were often used to symbolize love and freedom. It's a perfect gift for someone you care about—perhaps someone who is about to travel far away and needs a reminder of how much you care?

Instructions

Ribbing: With Black, CO 54 sts. Divide the sts onto 4 dpn. Join, being careful not to twist cast-on row. Work around in k1, p1 ribbing with 10 rnds Black, 2 rnds Rainbow, 4 rnds Black, 2 rnds Rainbow, 3 rnds Black. Finish with 1 knit rnd in Black.

1) After completing the ribbing, work following the chart for the respective right- or left-hand mitten (see page 93).

2) **Thumb Gusset:** Increase 2 sts on every other round as shown on the chart. When all the increases have been made, there should be a total of 64 sts around.

3) **Thumbhole:** The thick line on the chart indicates the placement of the thumbhole. Knit the 11 sts for the thumb with a smooth contrast color scrap yarn. Slide the sts back to the left needle and knit in pattern.

4) At the chart row with an encircled 4, continue the left and right mittens from the same chart.

5) Continue following the chart up to the encircled 5, and then shape top by decreasing as shown on the chart.

6) When 6 sts each remain on the front and back, seam the sets of stitches with Kitchener stitch.

7) **Thumb:** Insert a dpn into the sts below the scrap yarn and another dpn into the sts above the scrap yarn. Remove the scrap yarn = 11 + 11 sts. On the first rnd of the thumb, increase to 26 sts total by picking up and knitting 2 sts at each side (see chart).

8) Work thumb to encircled 8, and then shape top as shown on chart.

9) When 6 sts remain, cut yarn and draw end through rem sts. Weave in all yarn ends neatly on WS.

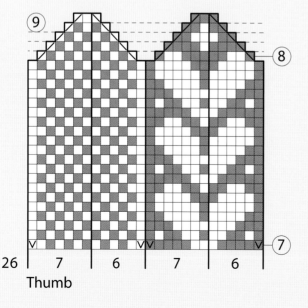

Thumb

26 | 7 | 6 | 7 | 6

		Knit
☐	▨	Knit
☐	▨	Purl
☑	☑	Increase 1 st
☑	◪	Right-leaning decrease
◸	◨	Left-leaning decrease

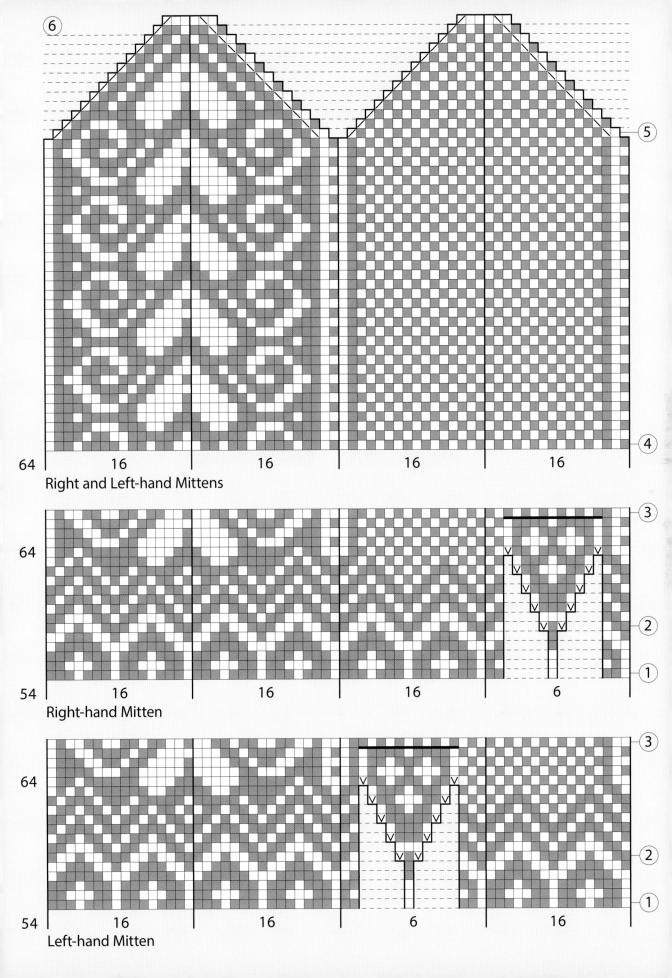

6

5

4

64   16   16   16   16

Right and Left-hand Mittens

3

2

1

64

54   16   16   16   6

Right-hand Mitten

3

2

1

64

54   16   16   6   16

Left-hand Mitten

KNOT

MATERIALS

Yarn: CYCA #1 (sock/fingering/baby) Sandnes Garn Sisu (80% wool, 20% nylon; 191 yd/175 m / 50 g), Charcoal #1088 and Gray Heather #1042

Needles: U.S. size 2.5 / 3 mm, set of 5 dpn

The motif for these mittens is the so-called "endless knot," a design element with many variations that's used in many different cultures and time periods. You can find similar knots, appropriate for both men and women, on wood carvings, gold work, and in book printing.

The Vikings often decorated their items with complex knots. The pattern for the Knot mittens is far from complex, as you'll see once you start knitting. These mittens are especially striking knitted in a yarn that has a rustic feel.

Instructions

Both mittens are worked the same way except for the thumb placement and the slant of the lines on each thumb.

With Charcoal (darkest color), CO 56 sts. Divide the sts onto 4 dpn. Join, being careful not to twist cast-on row.

1) Work following the chart for the right- and left-hand mittens (see page 96).

2) **Cuff:** (K2 with Gray, p2 with Charcoal) around. Work a total of 18 rnds ribbing.

3) Increase 12 sts as shown on the chart = 68 sts = 17 sts per dpn.

4) **Thumbhole:** The thick line on the chart (blue for left-hand and red for right) indicates the placement of the thumbhole. Knit the 12 sts for the thumb with a smooth contrast color scrap yarn. Slide the sts back to the left needle and knit in pattern.

5) Continue following the chart up to the encircled 4, and then shape top by decreasing as shown on the chart.

6) When 8 sts remain, cut yarn and draw end through rem sts.

7) **Thumb:** Insert a dpn into the sts below the scrap yarn and another dpn into the sts above the scrap yarn. Remove the scrap yarn = 12 + 12 sts. On the first rnd of the thumb, increase to 28 sts total by picking up and knitting 2 sts at each side (see chart). Be sure and work the correct thumb chart for each hand. The chart shows half the total sts—front and back of thumb are alike.

8) Work thumb to encircled 7, and then shape top as shown on chart.

9) When 8 sts remain, cut yarn and draw end through rem sts. Weave in all yarn ends neatly on WS.

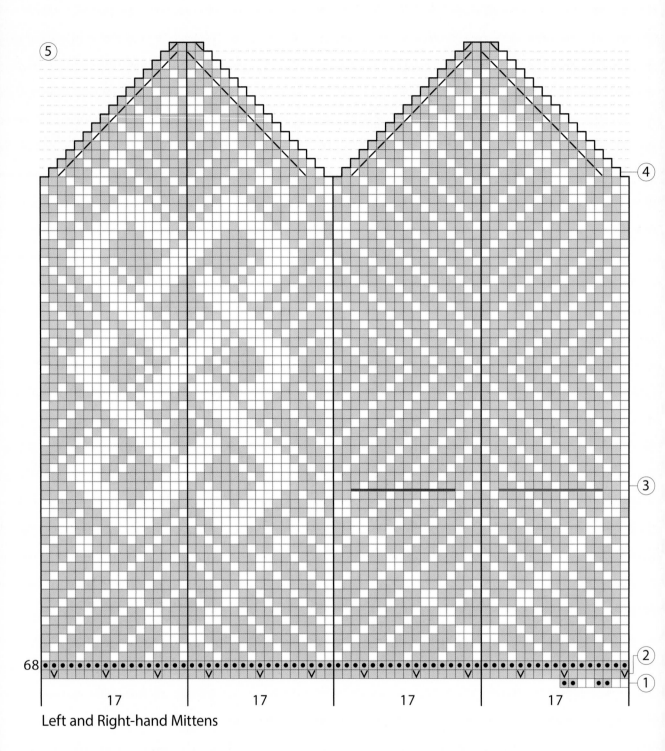

Left and Right-hand Mittens

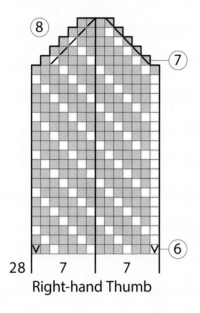

Right-hand Thumb

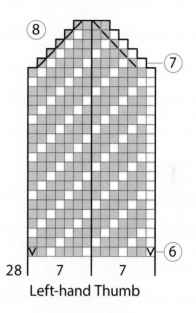

Left-hand Thumb

□ □ Knit
■ Purl
Ⅴ Ⅴ Increase 1 st
◨ ◩ Right-leaning decrease
◲ ◱ Left-leaning decrease

MITTENS FROM THE WILDERNESS

Anyone who walks in the woods or countryside will eventually meet some wild animals. Foxes, roe deer, squirrels, frogs, and salamanders are pleasant acquaintances and not usually very dangerous. It would be a little worse to come upon a large moose, not to mention the world's largest predator, a polar bear. But they are all totally safe on mittens—and, of course, quite decorative!

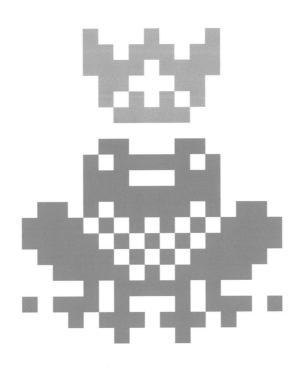

FOX

MATERIALS
Yarn: CYCA #1 (sock/fingering/baby) Rauma Finullgarn (100% wool; 191 yd/175 m / 50 g), Natural White #401 and Rust Red #435
Needles: U.S. size 1.5 / 2.5 mm, set of 5 dpn

The fox, with its cheery look and cunning spirit, is the source of numerous proverbs, stories, and songs. The images on these mittens are inspired by two of Aesop's fables: on the left-hand mitten, the fox tricks the crow into dropping its food by asking it to sing. On the right-hand mitten, the fox can't reach the fruit hanging high above him, and decides it's probably sour anyway—this story is where we get the expression "sour grapes"!

These mittens are loose-fitting and sized for adults.

Instructions

With White, CO 52 sts. Divide the sts evenly onto 4 dpn (= 13 sts per ndl). Join, being careful not to twist cast-on row.

1) Begin by working the ribbing following the chart below. **NOTE:** Work Rnd 1 with k1, p1 ribbing in White for 6 rounds.

2) Work the k2, p2 ribbing round (marked by encircled 2) 13 times.

3) After completing the cuff, continue, following the chart for the left- or right-hand mitten respectively. On Rnd 1 (marked by the encircled 3), increase a total of 4 sts (one new st on each needle) = 56 sts.

4) **Thumb Gusset:** Increase 2 sts on every other round as shown on the chart. When all the increases have been made, there should be a total of 64 sts around.

5) **Thumbhole:** The thick line on the chart indicates the placement of the thumbhole. Knit the 13 sts for the thumb with a smooth contrast color scrap yarn. Slide the sts back to the left needle and knit in pattern.

6) Continue following the chart up to the encircled 6, and then shape top by decreasing as shown.

7) When 8 sts each remain on the front and back,

seam the sets of stitches with Kitchener stitch.

8) **Thumb:** Insert a dpn into the sts below the scrap yarn and another dpn into the sts above the scrap yarn. Remove the scrap yarn = 13 + 13 sts. On the first rnd of the thumb, increase to 28 sts total by picking up and knitting 1 st at each side (see chart).

9) Work thumb to encircled 9, and then shape top as shown on chart.

10) When 8 sts remain, cut yarn and draw end through rem sts. Weave in all yarn ends neatly on WS.

Ribbing

		Knit
		Purl
☑	☑	Increase 1 st
☑	☑	Right-leaning decrease
◩	◩	Left-leaning decrease

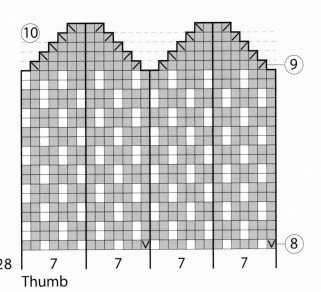

Thumb

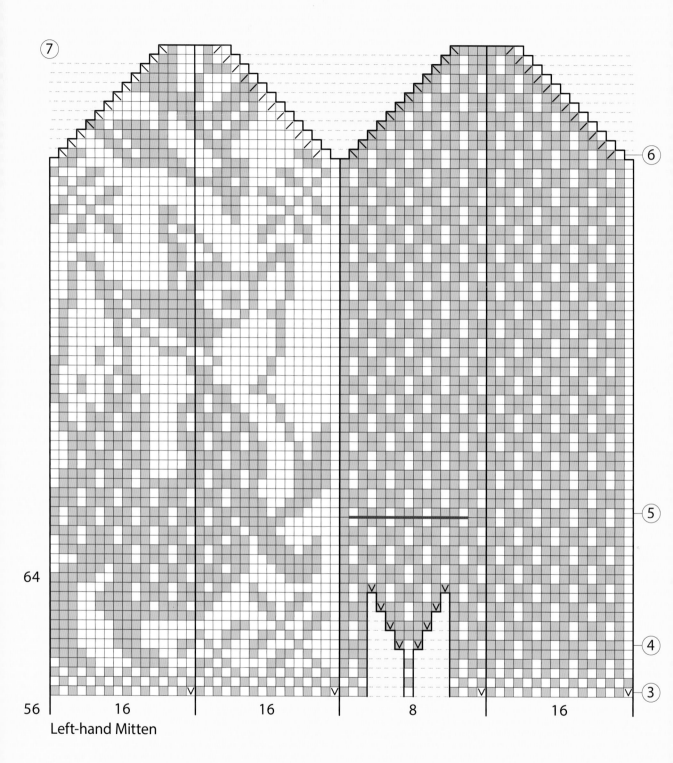

⑥

⑤

⑤

⑥

64

⑤

④

③

56

16   16   8   16

Left-hand Mitten

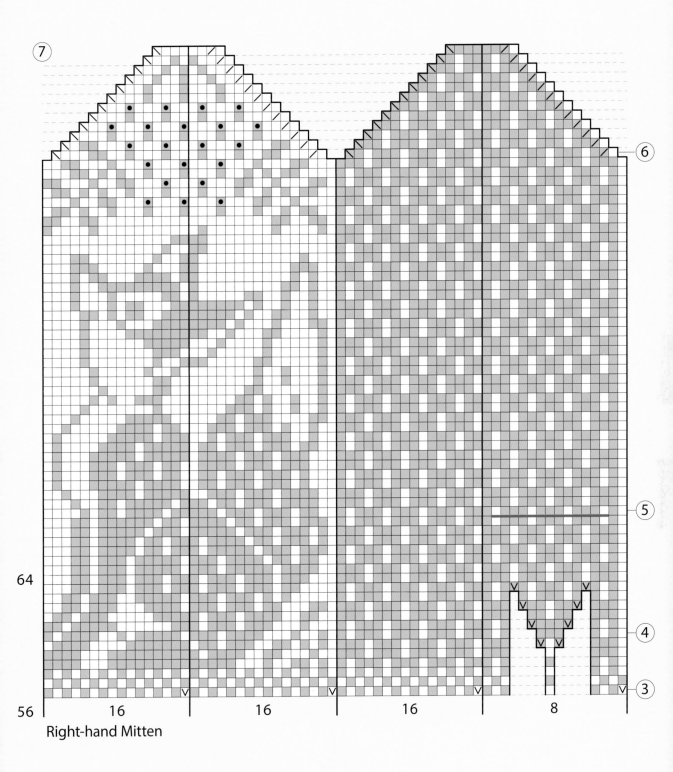

Right-hand Mitten

56 · · · 16 · · · 16 · · · 16 · · · 8

LITTLE FOX

MATERIALS

Yarn: CYCA #1 (sock/
fingering/baby) Rauma
Finullgarn (100% wool;
191 yd/175 m / 50 g),
Natural White #401
and Rust Red #435

Needles: U.S. size 1.5 /
2.5 mm, set of 5 dpn

The mother fox has had her pups—they're
running all around and leaving their paw
prints everywhere. These mittens are perfect
for the "paws" of little children who are always getting up to tricks!

The same pattern can easily be used for
larger or smaller children's sizes (see the ta-
bles on pages 13-17).

Instructions

With White, CO 44 sts. Divide the sts evenly onto 4 dpn (= 11 sts per ndl). Join, being careful not to twist cast-on row.

1) Begin by working the ribbing following the chart below. **NOTE:** Work Rnd 1 with k1, p1 ribbing in White for 4 rounds.

2) Repeat the k2, p2 ribbing round (marked by encircled 2) 10 times.

3) After completing the cuff, continue, following the chart for the left- or right-hand mitten respectively. On Rnd 1 (marked by the encircled 3), increase a total of 4 sts (one new st on each needle) = 48 sts.

4) **Thumbhole:** The thick line on the chart indicates the placement of the thumbhole. Knit the 9 sts for the thumb with a smooth contrast color scrap yarn. Slide the sts back to the left needle and knit in pattern.

5) Continue following the chart up to the encircled 5, and then shape top by decreasing as shown.

6) When 4 sts each remain on the front and back, cut yarn and draw end through rem sts.

7) **Thumb:** Insert a dpn into the sts below the scrap yarn and another dpn into the sts above the scrap yarn. Remove the scrap yarn = 9 + 9 sts. On the first rnd of the thumb, increase to 20 sts total by picking up and knitting 1 st at each side (see chart). The chart shows half the total sts—front and back of thumb are alike.

8) Work thumb to encircled 8, and then shape top as shown on chart.

9) When 6 sts remain, cut yarn and draw end through rem sts. Weave in all yarn ends neatly on WS.

Ribbing

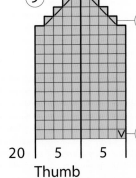

20 | 5 | 5

Thumb

		Knit
▪	▫	Purl
☑		Increase 1 st
◪	◹	Right-leaning decrease
◩	◺	Left-leaning decrease

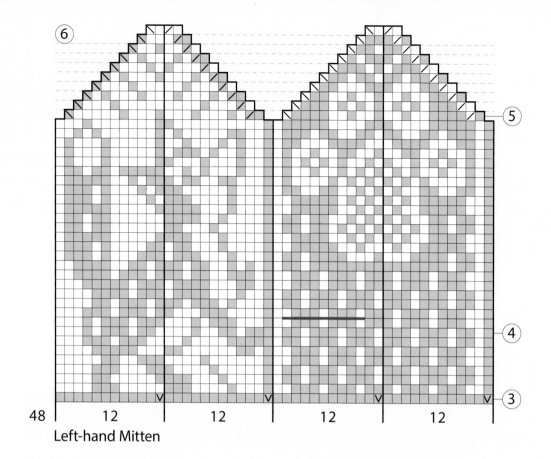

⑥

⑤

④

③

48 | 12 | 12 | 12 | 12 |

Left-hand Mitten

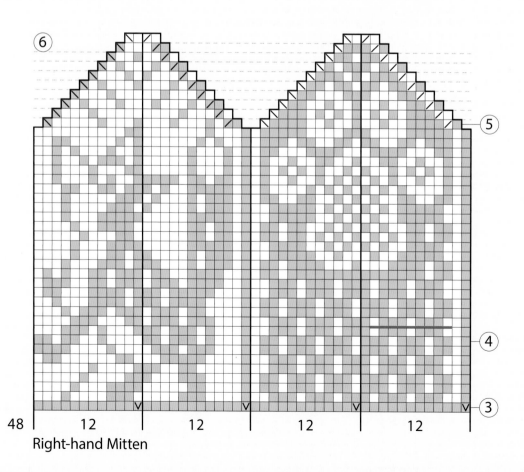

⑥

⑤

④

③

48 | 12 | 12 | 12 | 12 |

Right-hand Mitten

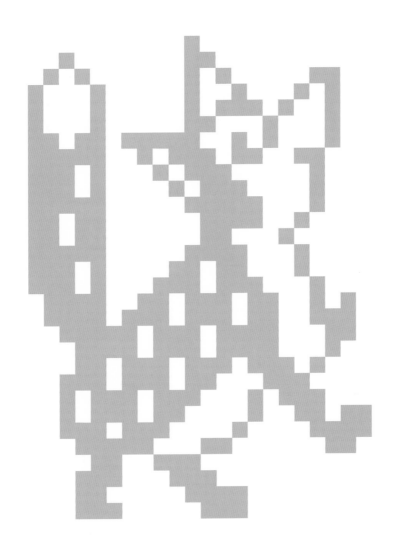

THE MOOSE HUNTERS

MATERIALS
Yarn: CYCA #2 (sport/baby) Dale Garn Falk (100% wool; 116 yd/106 m / 50 g), Light Beige #2642, Orange #3418, and Black #0090
Needles: U.S. size 2.5 / 3 mm, set of 5 dpn
Size: Men's

Knit these mittens for someone who loves to hunt. Who knows, maybe they'll bring a little extra luck! These mittens are a series of sketches, a hunting scene with dogs and a moose. Will the dogs ever catch the moose they're following?

These mittens will be even better once they're covered in evergreen needles and have all kinds of wear from the woods and countryside. Be sure and knit them with yarn that will tolerate heavy use.

Instructions

Ribbing: With Orange, CO 56 sts. Divide the sts onto 4 dpn = 14 sts per dpn. Join, being careful not to twist cast-on row. Work 6 rnds of k2, p2 ribbing and then continue in ribbing with (2 rnds Black, 3 rnds Orange) 3 times. Cut orange. Knit 1 rnd with Black.

1) Work following the chart for the right- or left-hand mitten respectively (see pages 112-113). On Rnd 1, increase 2 sts as indicated on the chart = 58 sts.

2) Thumb gusset increases: Increase 1 st at the side (see chart) on every other rnd until there are 64 sts total.

3) **Thumbhole:** The thick line on the chart indicates the placement of the thumbhole. Knit the 11 sts for the thumb with a smooth contrast color scrap yarn. Slide the sts back to the left needle and knit in pattern.

4) Continue following the chart up to the encircled 4, and then shape top by decreasing as shown on the chart.

5) When 8 sts remain, cut yarn and draw end through rem sts.

6) **Thumb:** Insert a dpn into the sts below the scrap yarn and another dpn into the sts above the scrap yarn. Remove the scrap yarn = 11 + 11 sts. On the first rnd of the thumb, increase to 26 sts total by picking up and knitting 2 sts at each side (see chart).

7) Work thumb to encircled 7 and then shape top as shown on chart.

8) When 6 sts remain, cut yarn and draw end through rem sts. Weave in all yarn ends neatly on WS.

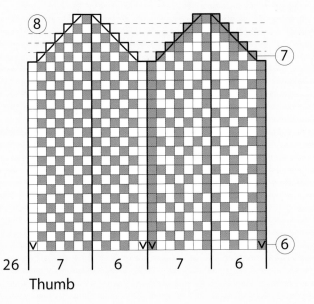

Thumb

		Knit
		Increase 1 st
		Right-leaning decrease
		Left-leaning decrease

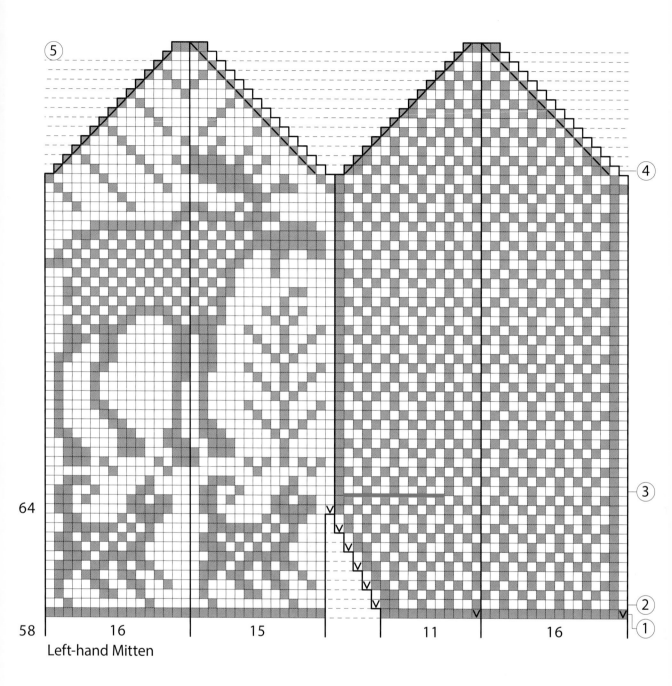

5

4

3

64

2

1

58

16   15   11   16

Left-hand Mitten

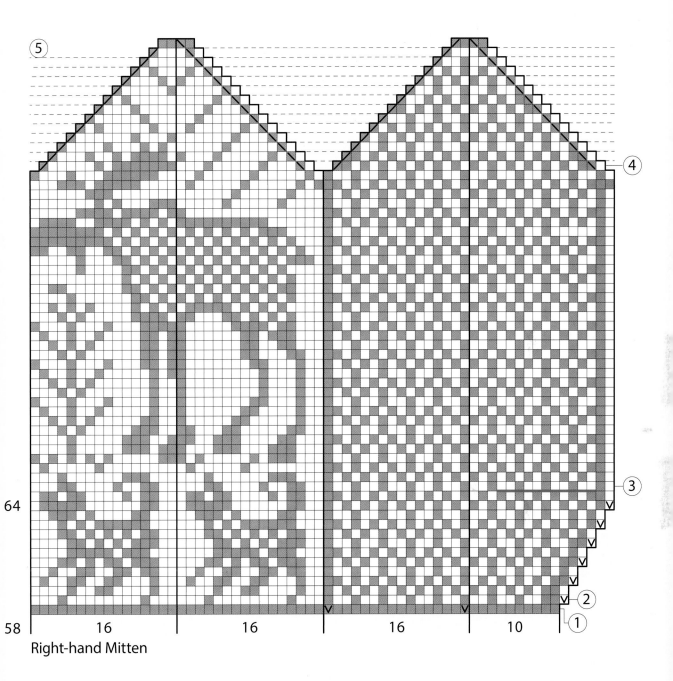

⑤

④

③

② 64

① 58

16   16   16   10

Right-hand Mitten

ROE DEER FAWN

MATERIALS

Yarn: CYCA #1 (sock/fingering/baby) Dale Garn Babyull (100% wool; 180 yd/165 m / 50 g), White #0010 and Beige Heather #3841

Needles: U.S. size 1.5 / 2.5 mm, set of 5 dpn

This fawn is still so young that it has white spots in the fur on its back. They are also on these mittens, which are sized for little hands. A bird has landed on the fawn's back—maybe it wants to share a secret? There's nothing to stop a bird and a fawn from becoming friends!

The mittens can be worked in several children's sizes, all from the same pattern (see the overview of sizing on page 12).

Instructions

With Beige, CO 44 sts. Divide the sts evenly onto 4 dpn (= 11 sts per ndl). Join, being careful not to twist cast-on row.

1) Begin by working the ribbing following the chart below; repeat two-stitch pattern around.

2) After completing the ribbing, knit 1 rnd with Beige Heather, and, on the chart row marked with an encircled 2, increase to 48 sts (increase 1 st on each dpn) = 12 sts per dpn

3) Continue, following the chart for the respective left- or right-hand mitten.

4) **Thumbhole:** The thick line on the chart indicates the placement of the thumbhole. Knit the 9 sts for the thumb with a smooth contrast color scrap yarn. Slide the sts back to the left needle and knit in pattern.

5) Continue following the chart up to the encircled 5, and then shape top by decreasing as shown.

6) When 4 sts each remain on the front and back, cut yarn and draw end through rem sts.

7) **Thumb:** Insert a dpn into the sts below the scrap yarn and another dpn into the sts above the scrap yarn. Remove the scrap yarn = 9 + 9 sts. On the first rnd of the thumb, increase to 22 sts total by picking up and knitting 2 sts at each side (see chart).

8) Work thumb to encircled 8, and then shape top as shown on chart.

9) When 6 sts remain, cut yarn and draw end through rem sts. Weave in all yarn ends neatly on WS.

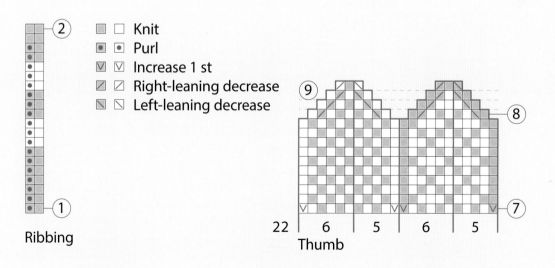

Knit

Purl

Increase 1 st

Right-leaning decrease

Left-leaning decrease

Ribbing

Thumb

22   6   5   6   5

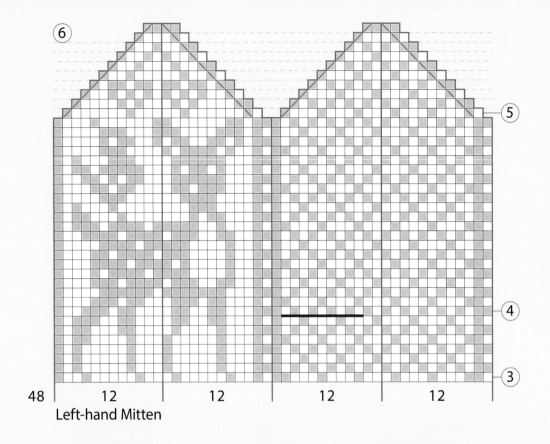

Left-hand Mitten

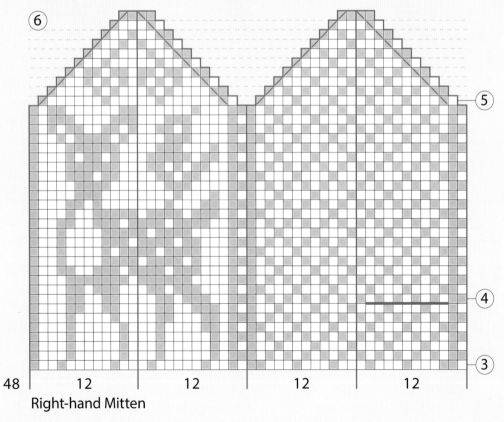

Right-hand Mitten

LITTLE SQUIRREL

MATERIALS

Yarn: CYCA #1 (sock/fingering/baby) Rauma Finullgarn (100% wool; 191 yd/175 m / 50 g), Rust Red #435, Green #432, and Natural White #401

Needles: U.S. size 2.5 / 3 mm, set of 5 dpn

Crochet Hook: U.S. size D / 3 mm for crocheted cords

The little squirrel hops around looking for nuts in the twigs and moss.

These children's mittens are knitted in a soft wool yarn. The loose shaping is cinched with a cord at the wrist.

Instructions

With Green, CO 48 sts. Divide the sts evenly onto 4 dpn (= 12 sts per ndl). Join, being careful not to twist cast-on row.

1) Begin by working the cuff following the chart below. The repeats are worked around.

2) At chart row marked by encircled 2, work the lace eyelets for the cord: (K1, p1, k2tog, yo) around. Continue up chart.

3) After completing the cuff, work following the chart for the respective left- or right-hand mitten. Cut Green and add Rust.

4) **Thumbhole:** The thick line on the chart indicates the placement of the thumbhole. Knit the 9

sts for the thumb with a smooth contrast color scrap yarn. Slide the sts back to the left needle and knit in pattern.

5) Continue following the chart up to the encircled 5, and then shape top by decreasing as shown.

6) When 5 sts each remain on the front and back, seam the sets of stitches with Kitchener st.

7) **Thumb:** Insert a dpn into the sts below the scrap yarn and another dpn into the sts above the scrap yarn. Remove the scrap yarn = 9 + 9 sts. On the first rnd of the thumb, increase to 22 sts total by picking up and knitting 2 sts at each side (see chart).

8) Work thumb to encircled 8, and then shape top as shown on chart.

9) When 6 sts remain, cut yarn and draw end through rem sts. Weave in all yarn ends neatly on WS. Make cords and draw through eyelet rounds as described below.

Cords (make 2): The cords in the pictures were crocheted with Green. Chain until cord is desired length. Turn and work 1 single crochet (British double crochet) in each chain st; fasten off. Draw cord through eyelet round so that the ends emerge at one side. The cord will roll nicely at the ends and stay in place even if the end unties.

▨	▧	☐	Knit
◉		⊡	Purl
⌒			Yarnover
	☑	☑	Increase 1 st
	▨	◪	Right-leaning decrease
◣	◹	◺	Left-leaning decrease

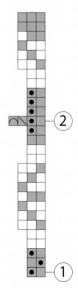

Chart 1

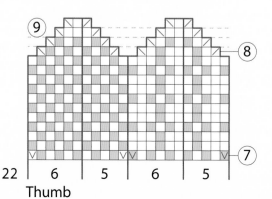

22 | 6 | 5 | 6 | 5

Thumb

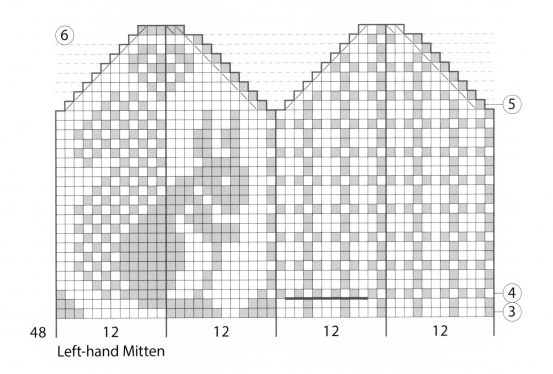

⑥

⑤

④
③

48 | 12 | 12 | 12 | 12 |

Left-hand Mitten

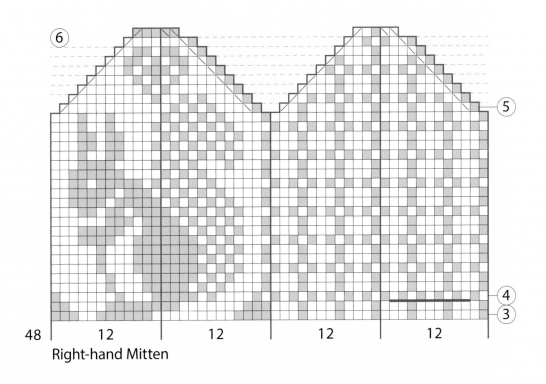

⑥

⑤

④
③

48 | 12 | 12 | 12 | 12 |

Right-hand Mitten

MOTHER SQUIRREL

MATERIALS

Yarn: CYCA #1 (sock/fingering/baby) Rauma Finullgarn (100% wool; 191 yd/175 m / 50 g), Rust Red #435, Green #432, and Natural White #401

Needles: U.S. size 2.5 / 3 mm, set of 5 dpn

Here in Norway there's a song about a young squirrel named Little Nut, who lives in the top of a tree and never gets anywhere on time. It's easy to be charmed by the lively and absent-minded Little Nut—and no one thinks about the poor mother squirrel and her daily fight to get the young ones where they should be! These mittens are designed to honor all the parents who manage these difficulties, especially those who feel they often barely make it. And who knows—perhaps these mittens will be the impetus for a little extra spring in your step.

Instructions

With White, CO 54 sts. Divide the sts onto 4 dpn. Join, being careful not to twist cast-on row.

1) Work following the chart for the respective right- or left-hand mitten (see pages 122-123). **NOTE:** Work 4 rnds of Rnd 1 (k1, p1 ribbing).

2) White and Rust Red stripes: Repeat this round (at encircled 2) 12 times.

3) Thumb gusset increases (beginning at encircled 3): Increase 1 st at the side (see chart) on every other rnd until there are 60 sts total.

4) **Thumbhole:** The thick line on the chart indicates the placement of the thumbhole. Knit the 11 sts for the thumb with a smooth contrast color scrap yarn. Slide the sts back to the left needle and knit in pattern.

5) Beginning at the chart row marked with an encircled 5, the mittens are worked the same way.

6) Continue following the chart up to the encircled 6, and then shape top by decreasing as shown on the chart.

7) When 7 sts each remain on the front and back, seam the sets of stitches with Kitchener st.

8) **Thumb:** Insert a dpn into the sts below the scrap yarn and another dpn into the sts above the scrap yarn. Remove the scrap yarn = 11 + 11 sts. On the first rnd of the thumb, increase to 26 sts total by picking up and knitting 2 sts at each side (see chart).

9) Work thumb to encircled 9, and then shape top as shown on chart.

10) When 6 sts remain, cut yarn and draw end through rem sts. Weave in all yarn ends neatly on WS.

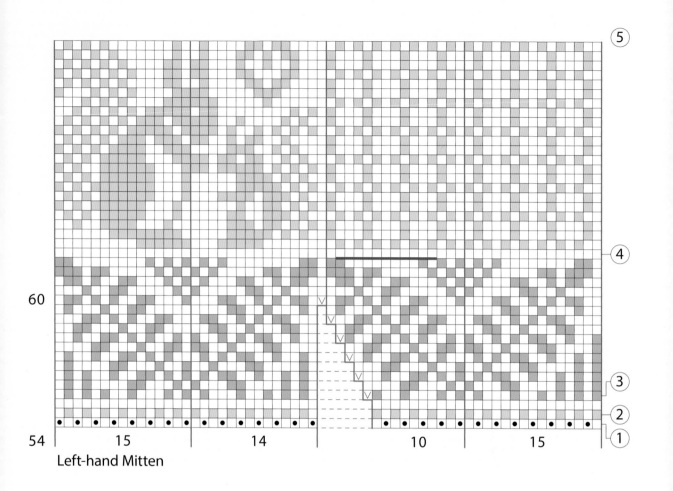

5

4

60

3

2

54

1

Left-hand Mitten

| 15 | 14 | 10 | 15 |

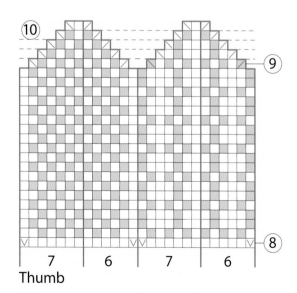

10

9

8

| 7 | 6 | 7 | 6 |

Thumb

Knit

• Purl

Increase 1 st

Right-leaning decrease

Left-leaning decrease

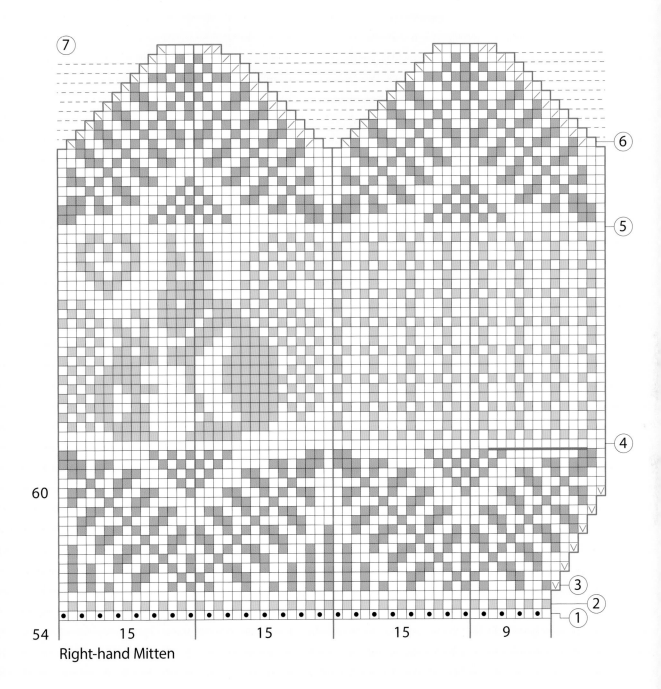

Right-hand Mitten

SANDRA SALAMANDER

MATERIALS

Yarn: CYCA #1 (sock/fingering/baby) Sandnes Garn Mini Alpakka (100% alpaca; 164 yd/150 m / 50 g), Petroleum #7212 and Black #1099; the zigzag is embroidered on after the mittens are knitted, using leftover yarn

Needles: U.S. size 2.5 / 3 mm, set of 5 dpn

The salamander has positioned itself in the center of the mitten and wound its long tail around the wrist. The design is eye-catching and was made precisely for anyone who longs for the unusual and likes to stand out a little.

Instructions

Both mittens are worked the same way except for the thumb placement and the slant of the lines on each thumb.

With Black, CO 60 sts. Divide the sts onto 4 dpn = 15 sts per dpn. Join, being careful not to twist cast-on row.

1) Work Chart 1 (repeating the four-stitch pattern around) up to the row marked with an encircled 2.

2) At the encircled 2, work the k2, p2 ribbing for 9 rounds.

3) After completing Chart 1 for the cuff, work following the chart for the right- and left-hand mittens respectively (see page 126).

4) **Thumbhole:** The thick line on the chart (blue line for left-hand and red for right) indicates the placement of the thumb-hole. Knit the 11 sts for the thumb with a smooth contrast color scrap yarn. Slide the sts back to the left needle and knit in pattern.

5) Continue following the chart up to the encircled 5, and then shape top by decreasing as shown on the chart.

6) When 8 sts remain, cut yarn and draw end through rem sts.

7) **Thumb:** Insert a dpn into the sts below the scrap yarn and another dpn into the sts above the scrap yarn. Remove the scrap yarn = 11 + 11 sts. On the first rnd of the thumb, increase to 26 sts total by picking up and knitting 2 sts at each side (see chart).

8) Work thumb to encircled 8, and then shape top as shown on chart.

9) When 6 sts remain, cut yarn and draw end through rem sts.

Weave in all yarn ends neatly on WS. Using duplicate stitch and dark pink or red yarn, embroider the zigzag over each salamander as shown in the drawing below. Weave in remaining ends on WS.

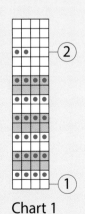

Chart 1

☐ ☐ Knit
⊡ ⊡ Purl
☑ ☑ Increase 1 st
◰ ◰ Right-leaning decrease
◱ ◱ Left-leaning decrease

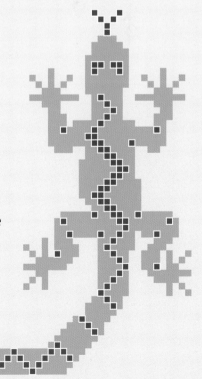

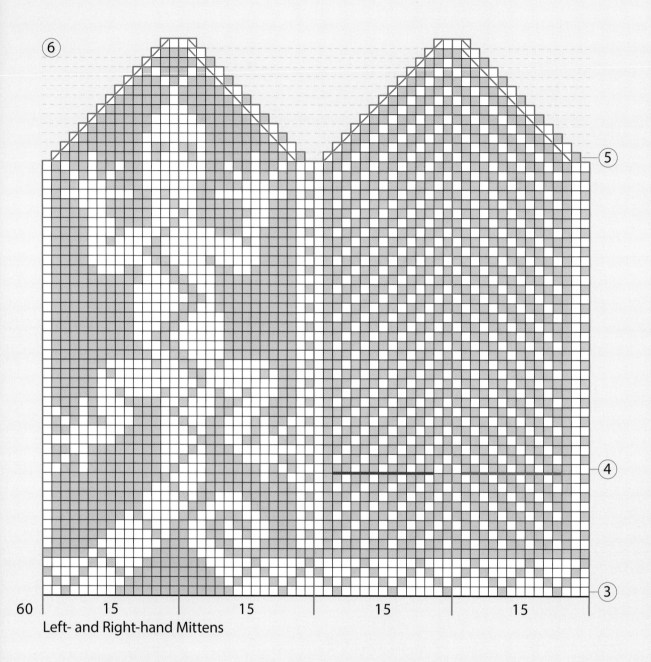

6

5

4

3

60 | 15 | 15 | 15 | 15 |

Left- and Right-hand Mittens

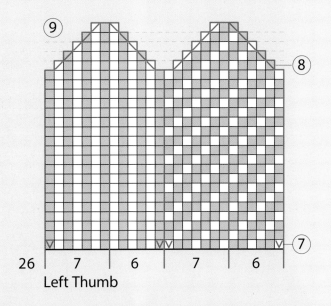

9

8

7

26 | 7 | 6 | 7 | 6

Left Thumb

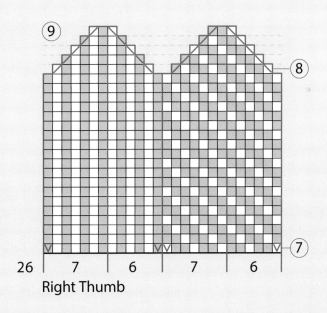

9

8

7

26 | 7 | 6 | 7 | 6

Right Thumb

DANCING FROGS

MATERIALS
Yarn: CYCA #1 (sock/fingering/baby) Du Store Alpakka Tynn Alpakka (100% alpaca; 183 yd/167 m / 50 g), Dark Turquoise #119 and Yellow-Green #116
Needles: U.S. size 2.5 / 3 mm, set of 5 dpn

The frog is an amusing fellow who jumps and hops—and dances. Have you ever come across a frog, hoping for a prince? Here's a possibility.

These mittens are long with nice lined cuffs. The attractive turn of the pattern on the cuffs stands out because it reverses the row sequence of the yarns on the back of the piece.

Instructions

Both mittens are worked the same way except for the thumb placement. Hold the yarns so the light color is dominant.

With Dark Turquoise, CO 60 sts. Divide the sts onto 4 dpn = 15 sts per dpn. Join, being careful not to twist cast-on row.

1) Work the cuff following the chart on page 130; the 4-stitch patterns are repeated around. Note details of cuff in Steps 2 and 3.

2) At the row marked with an encircled 2, purl around for the foldline.

3) At the encircled 3, hold the dark yarn as dominant for 3 rnds. Alternate the dominant yarn every three rounds to end of chart.

4) After completing cuff chart, work following the chart for the right- and left-hand mittens (see page 131).

5) **Thumbhole:** The thick line on the chart (blue for left-hand and red for right) indicates the placement of the thumb-hole. Knit the 11 sts for the thumb with a smooth contrast color scrap yarn. Slide the sts back to the left needle and knit in pattern.

6) Continue following the chart up to the encircled 7, and then shape top by decreasing as shown on the chart.

7) When 5 sts each remain on the front and back, seam the sets of stitches with Kitchener st.

8) **Thumb:** Insert a dpn into the sts below the scrap yarn and another dpn into the sts above the scrap yarn. Remove the scrap yarn = 11 + 11 sts. On the first rnd of the thumb, increase to 26 sts total by picking up and knitting 2 sts at each side (see chart).

9) Work thumb to encircled 10, and then shape top as shown on chart.

10) When 6 sts remain, cut yarn and draw end through rem sts.

Weave in all yarn ends neatly on WS. Fold the cuff lining in to WS and sew down loosely.

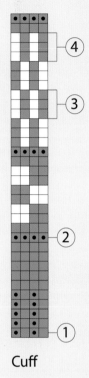

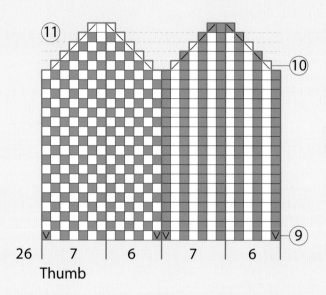

Cuff

Thumb

□ ■ Knit
· Purl
▼ Increase 1 st
◩ ◪ Right-leaning decrease
◨ � Left-leaning decrease

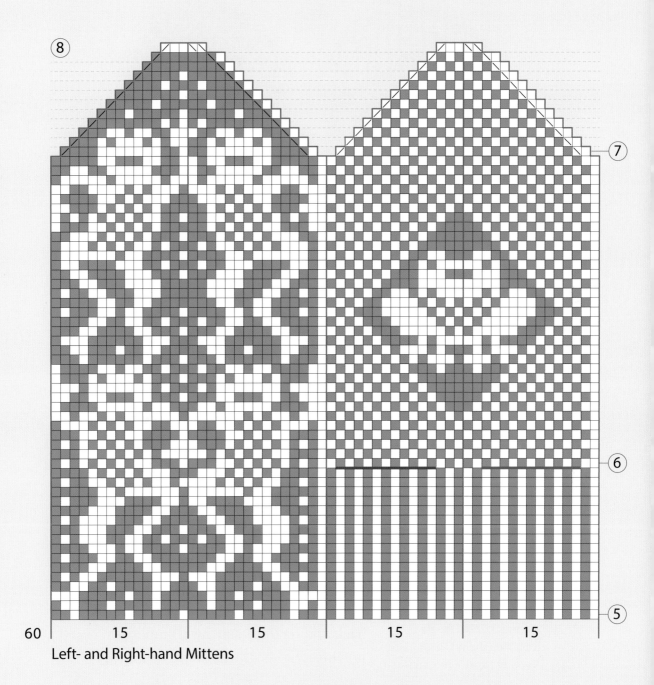

Left- and Right-hand Mittens

THE NORTH POLE

MATERIALS
Yarn: CYCA #1 (sock/fingering/baby) Viking of Norway Nordlys superwash (75% wool, 25% nylon; 382 yd/349 m / 100 g), Blue #927; CYCA #1 (sock/fingering/baby) Sandnes Garn Sisu (80% wool, 20% nylon; 191 yd/175 m / 50 g), White #1001
Needles: U.S. size 2.5 / 3 mm, set of 5 dpn

Up at the North Pole, polar bears shuffle back and forth under the glimmering northern lights. These large, beautiful animals walk over the ice in pairs with the heavens arched above them. The panel at the bottom of each mitten represents the open channels that break out between floes of ice and snow.

Instructions

With Blue, CO 56 sts. Divide the sts onto 4 dpn = 14 sts per dpn. Join, being careful not to twist cast-on row.

1) Work following Chart 1, working the repeats around. Work to encircled 2.

2) At the chart row marked with an encircled 2, increase 1 st on each needle = 60 sts.

3) After completing Chart 1, work following the chart for the right- or left-hand mitten respectively (see pages 134-135).

4) **Thumbhole:** The thick line on the chart indicates the placement of the thumbhole. Knit the 11 sts for the thumb with a smooth contrast color scrap yarn. Slide the sts back to the left needle and knit in pattern.

5) Continue following the chart up to the encircled 5, and then shape top by decreasing as shown on the chart.

6) When 7 sts each remain on the front and back, seam the sets of stitches with Kitchener stitch.

7) **Thumb:** Insert a dpn into the sts below the scrap yarn and another dpn into the sts above the scrap yarn. Remove the scrap yarn = 11 + 11 sts. On the first rnd of the thumb, increase to 26 sts total by picking up and knitting 2 sts at each side (see chart).

8) Work thumb to encircled 8, and then shape top as shown on chart.

9) When 6 sts remain, cut yarn and draw end through rem sts. Weave in all yarn ends neatly on WS.

		Knit
▨	☐	
	•	Purl
☑	☑	Increase 1 st
◪	◿	Right-leaning decrease
◩	◺	Left-leaning decrease

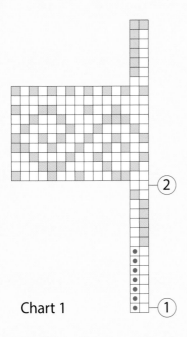

Chart 1

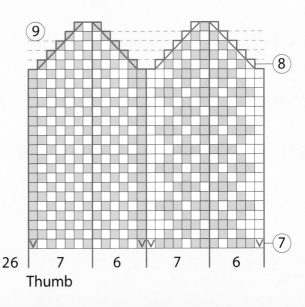

Thumb

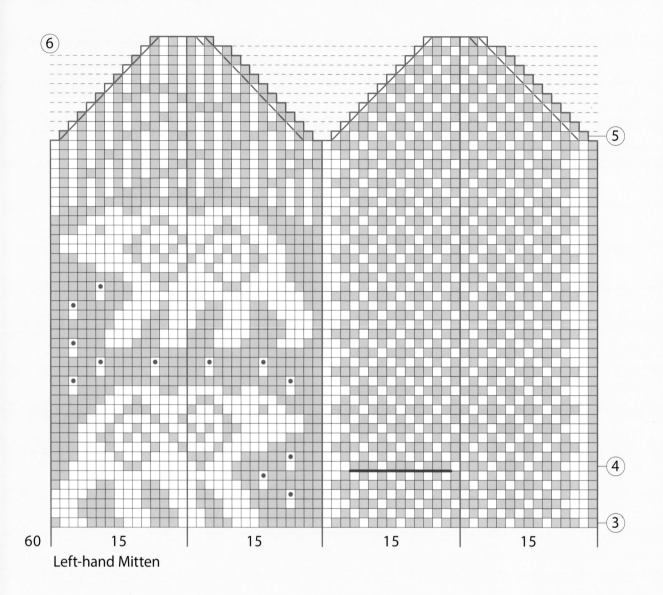

60

15 15 15 15

Left-hand Mitten

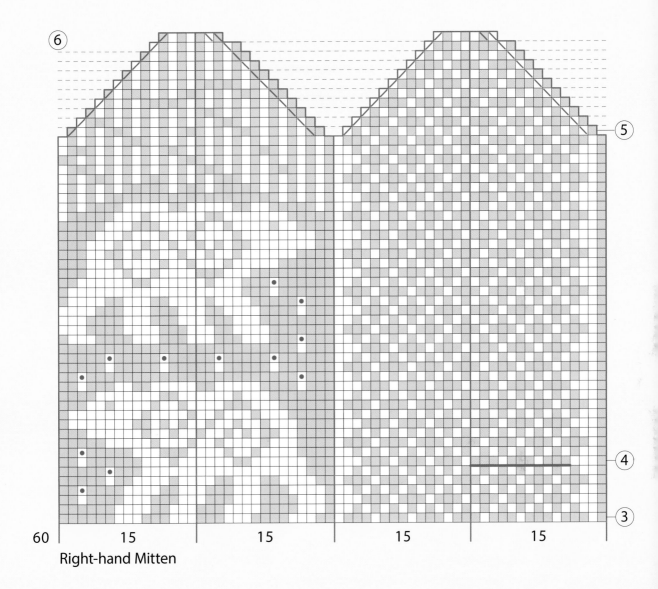

Right-hand Mitten

DOMESTIC ANIMALS

Where would we be without our domestic animals? The next section features mittens with motifs from the cowshed, horse stall, and fields, to honor our good domestic animals. The reindeer is also included, although they live outdoors.

HORSE-HAPPINESS AND LUCK

MATERIALS
Yarn: CYCA #1 (sock/fingering/baby) Rauma Finullgarn (100% wool; 191 yd/175 m / 50 g), Light Gray #403, Black #436, and Orange #461
Needles: U.S. size 2.5 / 3 mm, set of 5 dpn

Horses are high on the wishlist of many people, so here's a pair of mittens for those who find happiness in the riding barn. A proud horse dashingly rears up on two legs; the four-leaf clover on the mitten palm will bring prosperity and luck to any rider.

Instructions

With Light Gray, CO 56 sts. Divide the sts onto 4 dpn = 14 sts per ndl. Join, being careful not to twist cast-on row.

1) Work following the chart for the lower edge. The two-stitch pattern repeats around.

2) On the chart row marked with an encircled 2, increase 1 st on each needle = 60 sts (and 15 sts per dpn).

3) After completing the lower edge chart, continue to the chart or the respective right- or left-hand mitten (see pages 140-141). If you like, substitute a heart panel or your own design for the text "Horse = luck." You'll find charted alphabets on page 214.

4) **Thumbhole:** The thick line on the chart indicates the placement of the thumbhole. Knit the 11 sts for the thumb with a smooth contrast color scrap yarn. Slide the sts back to the left needle and knit in pattern.

5) Starting at the chart row marked with an encircled 5, shape top by decreasing as shown on the chart.

6) When 7 sts each remain on the front and back, seam the sets of stitches with Kitchener st.

7) **Thumb:** Insert a dpn into the sts below the scrap yarn and another dpn into the sts above the scrap yarn. Remove the scrap yarn = 11 + 11 sts. On the first rnd of the thumb, increase to 26 sts total by picking up and knitting 2 sts at each side (see chart).

8) Work thumb to encircled 8, and then shape top as shown on chart.

9) When 6 sts remain, cut yarn and draw end through rem sts. Weave in all yarn ends neatly on WS.

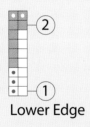

Lower Edge

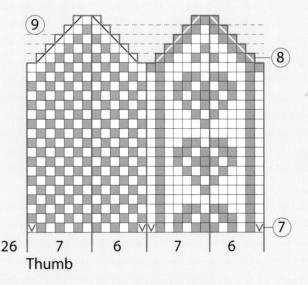

Thumb

26 | 7 | 6 | 7 | 6

- ▨ ▨ □ Knit
- ▣ ⊡ Purl
- ☑ Increase 1 st
- ▨ ☑ Right-leaning decrease
- ▨ ◩ Left-leaning decrease

⑥

⑤

④

③

60   15   15   15   15

Left-hand Mitten

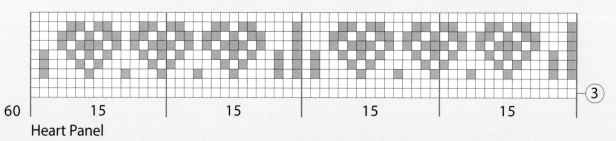

③

60   15   15   15   15

Heart Panel

⑥

⑤

④

③

60   15   15   15   15

Right-hand Mitten

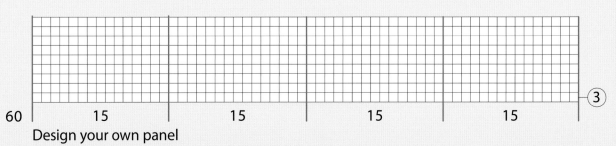

③

60   15   15   15   15

Design your own panel

COW MITTENS

MATERIALS
Yarn: CYCA #1 (sock/fingering/baby) Dale Garn Daletta (100% wool; 153 yd/140 m / 50 g), White #0010, Black #0090, and Light Green #9133 + small amounts of Powder Pink #4202 and Fuchsia #4516 for embroidery
Needles: U.S. size 2.5 / 3 mm, set of 5 dpn

It's not easy to arrange a cow motif on a mitten since mittens and cows are oriented differently! The cow doesn't mind, though; it goes where it goes and is reversed on each mitten. This cow stands in the middle of a flowering clover field. These charming cow mittens will bring out the sense of humor in most people and will be especially appropriate for anyone who, just like the cow, prefers to go where they please.

These mittens are knitted with black, white, and green yarn. You'll also need a little light and dark pink yarn for the embroidery.

Instructions

Both mittens are worked the same way except for the thumb placement and the thumb motifs. With Light Green, CO 60 sts. Divide the sts evenly onto 4 dpn (= 15 sts per ndl). Join, being careful not to twist cast-on row.

1) Work following Chart 1, repeating the two-stitch pattern around. Note details in steps 2–4.

2) White and Light Green stripes beginning at encircled 2: Hold the yarn so Light Green is dominant.

3) At the chart row marked with an encircled 3, hold the yarn so White is dominant.

4) At the chart row marked with an encircled 4, increase 1 st on each needle = 64 sts. From this point on, Light Green, and later Black, is dominant.

5) After completing Chart 1, work following the chart for the right- and left-hand mittens (see pages 144-145).

6) **Thumbhole:** The thick line on the chart indicates the placement of the thumbhole (blue line for left-hand mitten and red line for right mitten). Knit the 12 sts for the thumb with a smooth contrast color scrap yarn. Slide the sts back to the left needle and knit in pattern.

7) Continue following the chart up to the encircled 7; then cut Black and continue with Light Green and White only. Shape top by decreasing as shown on the chart.

8) When 8 sts remain, cut yarn and draw end through rem sts.

9) **Thumb:** Insert a dpn into the sts below the scrap yarn and another dpn into the sts above the scrap yarn. Remove the scrap yarn = 12 + 12 sts. On the first rnd of the thumb, increase to 28 sts total by picking up and knitting 2 sts at each side (see chart).

10) Work thumb to encircled 10, and then shape top as shown on chart.

11) When 8 sts remain, cut yarn and draw end through rem sts. Weave in all yarn ends neatly on WS.

Using duplicate stitch and Powder Pink, embroider the cow's udder, snout, and ears. With Fuchsia and Light Green, embroider the clover flowers and leaves. Weave in ends on WS.

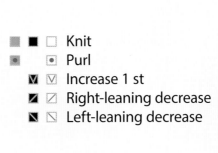

■ ■ □ Knit
■ ⊡ Purl
Ⓥ ☑ Increase 1 st
◪ ◿ Right-leaning decrease
◣ ◺ Left-leaning decrease

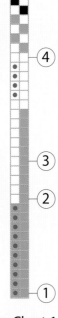

Chart 1

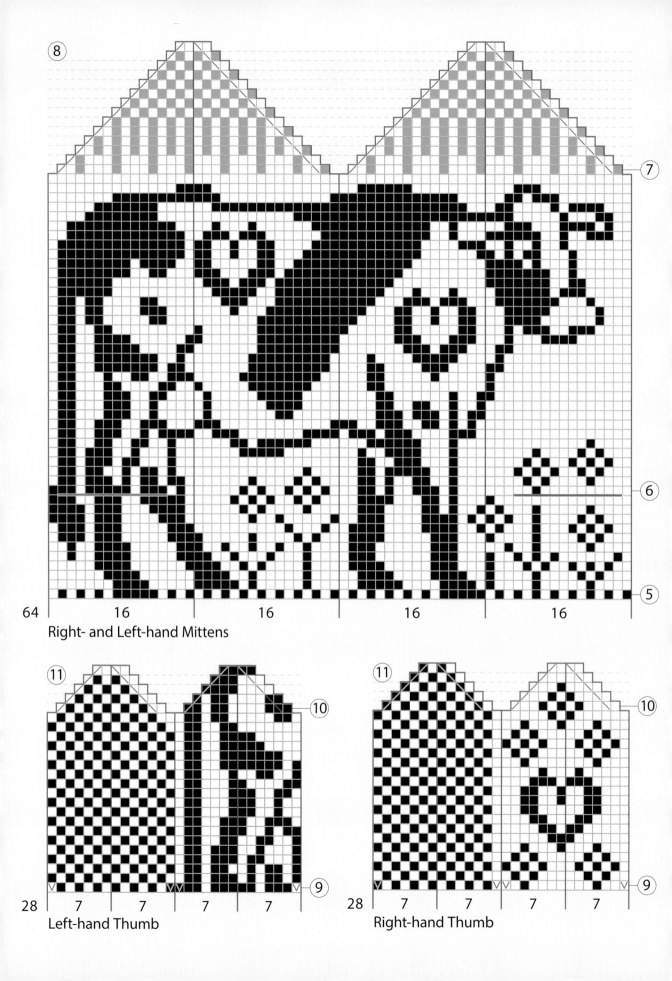

⑧

⑦

64   16   16   16   16
Right- and Left-hand Mittens

⑥

⑤

⑪   ⑪
        ⑩   ⑩

⑨   ⑨

28   7   7   28   7   7
Left-hand Thumb   Right-hand Thumb

Use Powder Pink, Fuchsia, and Light Green for embroidery on both mittens.

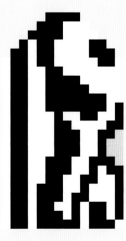

Left Thumb

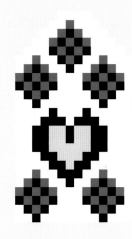

Right Thumb

CALF

MATERIALS

Yarn: CYCA #1 (sock/fingering/baby) Dale Garn Daletta (100% wool; 153 yd/140 m / 50 g), White #0010, Dark Brown #3695, and Light Green #9133 + small amount of Powder Pink #4202 for embroidery

Needles: U.S. size 2.5 / 3 mm, set of 5 dpn

Crochet Hook: U.S. size D / 3 mm for crocheted cords

Here are the sweet sister mittens to the Cow mittens. These mittens are for children who drink milk and who know what animal says MOO. I am positive that these mittens will make their owner very happy and will keep any little child's hands toasty warm.

Instructions

With White, CO 44 sts. Divide the sts evenly onto 4 dpn (= 11 sts per ndl). Join, being careful not to twist cast-on row.

1) Work following Chart 1 (see page 149), repeating the two-stitch pattern around.

2) Lace eyelet round (at end encircled 2; can be omitted if you don't want cord ties for the mittens): (K1 White, 1 Light Green yo, k2tog with White, k1 Light Green) around.

3) Continue to the chart for the right- or left-hand mitten respectively. Cut Light Green and add Dark Brown. As indicated on the first row of the chart, increase 1 st on each dpn = 48 sts.

4) **Thumbhole:** The thick line on the chart indicates the placement of the thumbhole. Knit the 9 sts for the thumb with a smooth contrast color scrap yarn. Slide the sts back to the left needle and knit in pattern.

5) Continue following the chart up to the encircled 5; cut Dark Brown and continue with Light Green and White only. Shape top by decreasing as shown on the chart.

6) When 5 sts each remain on the front and back, seam the sets of stitches with Kitchener stitch.

7) **Thumb:** Insert a dpn into the sts below the scrap yarn and another dpn into the sts above the scrap yarn. Remove the scrap yarn = 9 + 9 sts. On the first rnd of the thumb, increase to 22 sts total by picking up and knitting 2 sts at each side (see chart).

8) Work thumb to encircled 8, and then shape top as shown on chart.

9) When 6 sts remain, cut yarn and draw end through rem sts. Weave in all yarn ends neatly on WS.

10) Using duplicate stitch and Powder Pink, embroider the cow's snout and ears. Weave in ends on WS.

Cords (make 2): The cords in the pictures were crocheted with Light Green. Chain until cord is desired length. Turn and work 1 single crochet (British double crochet) in each chain st; fasten off. Draw cord through eyelet round so that the ends emerge at one side.

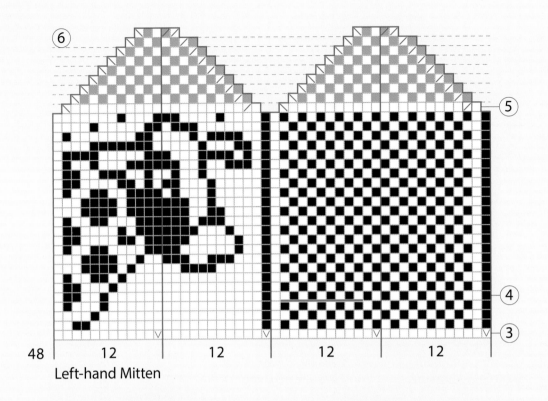

Left-hand Mitten

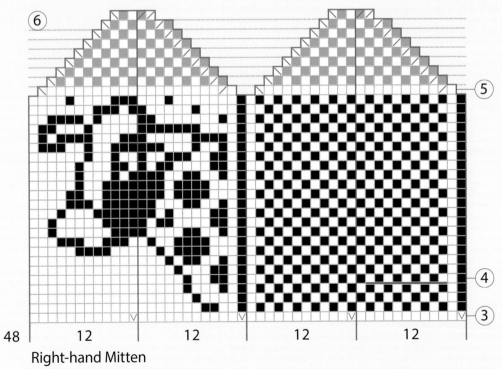

Right-hand Mitten

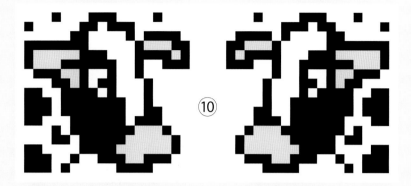

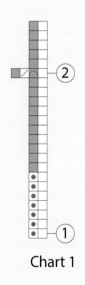

Chart 1

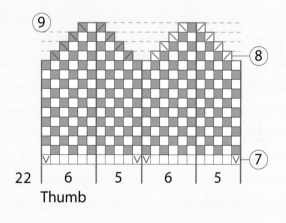

22   6   5   6   5

Thumb

■ ▨ □ Knit
⊡ Purl
◨ Yarnover
☑ Increase 1 st
▨ ☑ Right-leaning decrease
▨ ◩ Left-leaning decrease

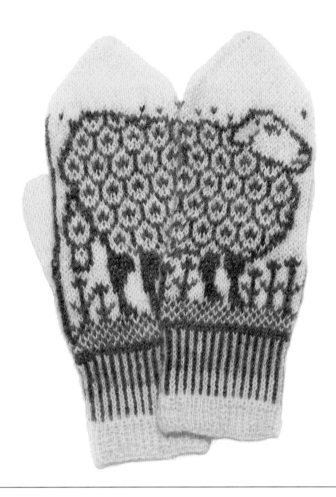

SHEEP MITTENS

MATERIALS
Yarn: CYCA #1 (sock/fingering/baby) Du Store Alpakka Tynn Alpakka (100% alpaca; 183 yd/167 m / 50 g), White #101 and Gray #114; small amount of Red #130; CYCA #1 (sock/fingering/baby) Drops Alpaca (100% alpaca; 182 yd/166 m / 50 g) Green #2916
Needles: U.S. size 2.5 / 3 mm, set of 5 dpn

The sheep is an important domestic animal—without sheep, we wouldn't be able to knit such lovely, warm woolen mittens. As with the cows, the sheep spans the mittens, calmly grazing in the flowers and green grass.

These mittens are carefully designed with many small details to make them extra nice.

The colors of the flowers and the sheep's nose and ears are embroidered on afterwards with duplicate stitch. The thumbs and white tops of the mittens are worked with two alternating strands of white yarn.

Instructions

With White, CO 58 sts. Divide the sts onto 4 dpn. Join, being careful not to twist cast-on row.

1) Work the cuff following Chart 1 on page 152; repeat two-stitch pattern around. Note details in Steps 2–4.

2) Green and White stripes on the chart rows indicated by the encircled 2: Hold the yarn so that the White is dominant.

3) At the encircled 3, hold the green yarn as dominant. For the remainder of the mitten, either the Green or Gray should be dominant.

4) On the chart row marked with the encircled 4, increase 6 sts evenly spaced around = 64 sts / 16 sts on each dpn.

5) After completing chart 1, cut Green and continue with White and Gray only. Work following the chart for the right- and left-hand mittens (see page 152).

6) **Thumbhole:** The thick line on the chart (blue for left-hand and red for right) indicates the placement of the thumbhole. Knit the 12 sts for the thumb with a smooth contrast color scrap yarn. Slide the sts back to the left needle and knit in pattern.

7) In the section outlined by yellow-green and marked with an encircled 7, the sheep are worked differently for the right- and left-hand mittens. Be sure to follow the appropriate chart.

8) The top of each mitten is worked the same way with two strands of White: alternate the strands stitch to stitch.

9) Continue following the chart up to the encircled 9, and then shape top by decreasing as shown on the chart.

10) When 5 sts each remain on the front and

back, seam the sets of stitches with Kitchener st.

11) **Thumb:** Insert a dpn into the sts below the scrap yarn and another dpn into the sts above the scrap yarn. Remove the scrap yarn = 12 + 12 sts. On the first rnd of the thumb, increase to 28 sts total by picking up and knitting 2 sts at each side (see chart). Repeat the chart twice—the front and back of each thumb are the same.

12) Work thumb to encircled 12 and then shape top as shown on chart.

13) When 8 sts remain, cut yarn and draw end through rem sts. Weave in all yarn ends neatly on WS.

14) Using leftover pink yarn and duplicate stitch, embroider the sheep's ears and mouth. Embroider the flowers with Red and Green. Weave in all ends neatly on WS.

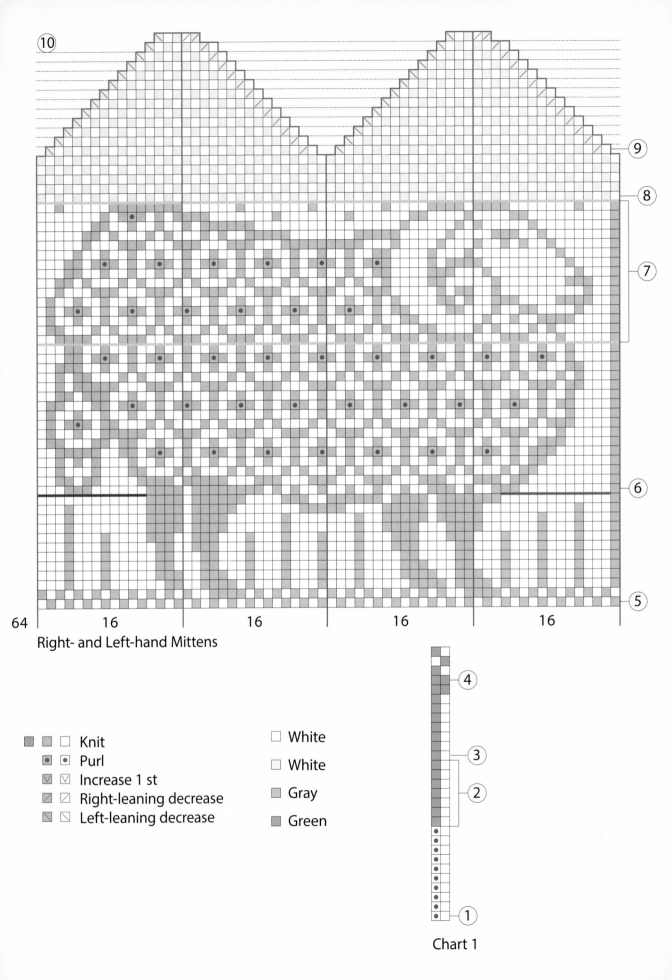

64

Right- and Left-hand Mittens

16 16 16 16

Knit
Purl
Increase 1 st
Right-leaning decrease
Left-leaning decrease

White
White
Gray
Green

Chart 1

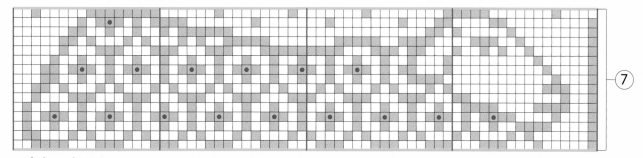

Left-hand Mitten

⑦

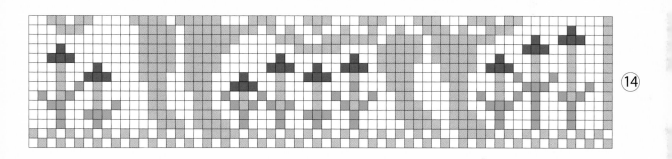

⑭

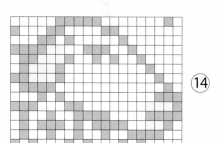

⑭

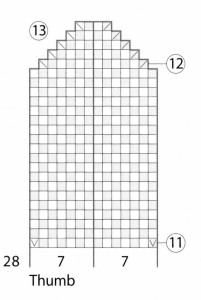

⑬

⑫

⑪

28 | 7 | 7

Thumb

REINDEER

MATERIALS
Yarn: CYCA #1 (sock/fingering/baby) Dale Garn Daletta (100% wool; 153 yd/140 m / 50 g), White #0010 and Blue #5436
Needles: U.S. size 2.5 / 3 mm, set of 5 dpn

Reindeer aren't really domestic animals, but many in Norway are taken care of by people, and there are lots of large herds of these lovely animals. A very proud reindeer elegantly raises his head in this motif. These mittens have a pretty palm pattern and a nicely placed thumb, with a good, old-fashioned cuff lining.

Instructions

These mittens are lined with a cuff facing that is folded in to the wrong side.

Facing: With White, CO 64 sts. Divide the sts evenly onto 4 dpn (= 16 sts per ndl). Join, being careful not to twist cast-on row. Work 10 rnds k1, p1 ribbing and then knit 5 rnds stockinette. Eyelet round (foldline): (K2tog, yo) around. Knit 3 rnds.

1) Work the charted pattern panel, repeating the 8-stitch pattern around.

2) At the chart row marked with an encircled 2, decrease 4 sts = 1 st on each dpn = 60 sts rem.

3) After completing the panel, work following the chart for the respective right- or left-hand mitten (see pages 156-157).

4) **Thumbhole:** The thick line on the chart indicates the placement of the thumbhole. Knit the 11 sts for the thumb with a smooth contrast color scrap yarn. Slide the sts back to the left needle and knit in pattern.

5) Continue following the chart up to the encircled 5, and then shape top by decreasing as shown on the chart.

6) When 8 sts remain, cut yarn and draw end through rem sts.

7) **Thumb:** Insert a dpn into the sts below the scrap yarn and another dpn into the sts above the scrap yarn. Remove the scrap yarn = 11 + 11 sts. On the first rnd of the thumb, increase to 26 sts total by picking up and knitting 2 sts at each side (see chart).

8) Work thumb to encircled 8, and then shape top as shown on chart.

9) When 6 sts remain, cut yarn and draw end through rem sts. Weave in all yarn ends neatly on WS.

Fold the lining at the eyelet round and sew down loosely on WS.

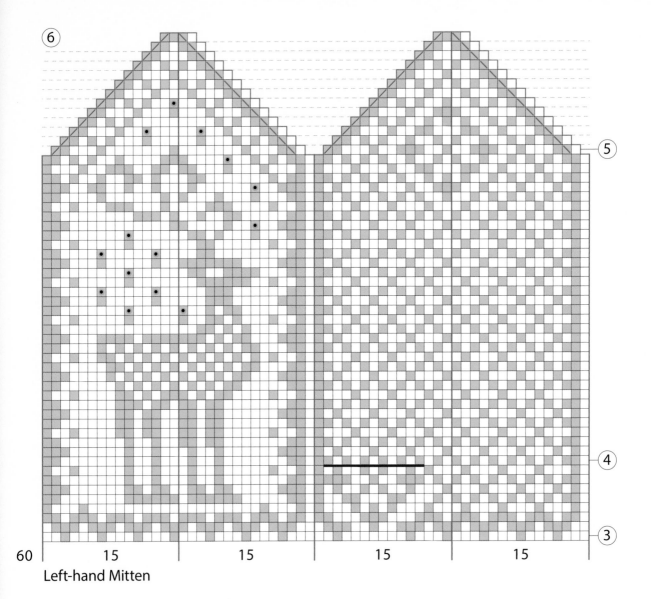

⑥

⑤

④

③

60 | 15   15   15   15

Left-hand Mitten

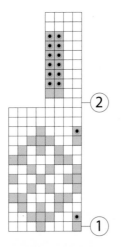

②

①

Pattern Panel

		Knit
●		Purl
⊻	⊻	Increase 1 st
◩	◪	Right-leaning decrease
◣	◺	Left-leaning decrease

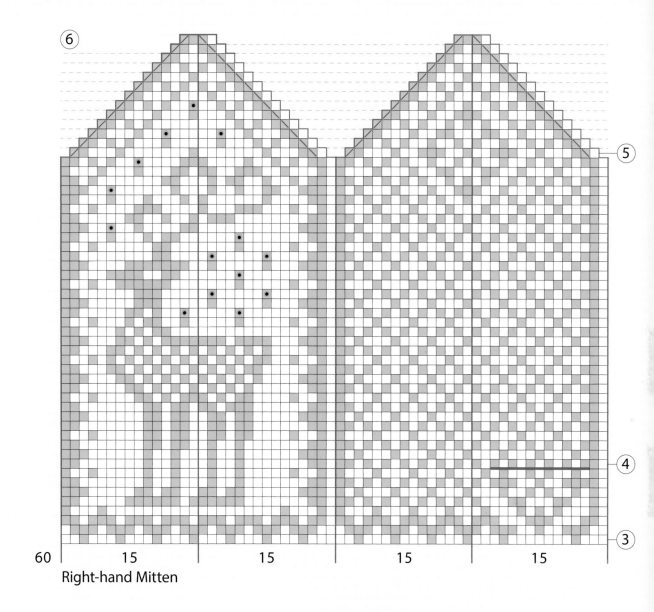

⑥

⑤

④

③

60   15   15   15   15

Right-hand Mitten

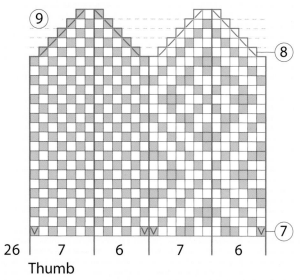

⑨

⑧

⑦

26   7   6   7   6

Thumb

LITTLE LAMB

MATERIALS
Yarn: CYCA #1 (sock/
fingering/baby) Dale
Garn Daletta (100% wool;
153 yd/140 m / 50 g),
Natural White #0020,
Light Green #9133, and
Lilac #5032
Needles: U.S. size 2.5 /
3 mm, set of 5 dpn

These little mittens are for anyone who likes
to sing "Mary Had A Little Lamb." The colors
were inspired by a lilac bush that blooms at
about the same time as the little lambs come
out onto the grass for the first time. Even if
you've put away your mittens for the season,
the little ones might need something warm
on their fingers when sitting in the stroller
on a chilly spring day.

Instructions

With White, CO 48 sts. Divide the sts evenly onto 4 dpn (= 12 sts per ndl). Join, being careful not to twist cast-on row.

1) Work following Chart 1, in ribbing and stripes; the patterns repeat around.

2) Lace eyelet round (at chart row with encircled 2; for tie cords): (K1, p1, k2tog, yo) around.

3) Continue to the chart for the right- or left-hand mitten respectively. Cut Lilac and add in Light Green.

4) **Thumbhole:** The thick line on the chart indicates the placement of the thumbhole. Knit the 7 sts for the thumb with a smooth contrast color scrap yarn. Slide the sts back to the left needle and knit in pattern.

5) Continue following the chart up to the encircled 5; shape top by decreasing as shown on the chart.

6) When 5 sts each remain on the front and back, seam the sets of stitches with Kitchener stitch.

7) **Thumb:** Insert a dpn into the sts below the scrap yarn and another dpn into the sts above the scrap yarn. Remove the scrap yarn = 7 + 7 sts. On the first rnd of the thumb, increase to 18 sts total by picking up and knitting 2 sts at each side (see chart).

8) Work thumb to encircled 8, and then shape top as shown on chart.

9) When 6 sts remain, cut yarn and draw end through rem sts. Weave in all yarn ends neatly on WS.

Twist yarns for the cord and draw through eyelet round. To twist cords, cut strands of Lilac and White (as pictured here) about 3 times longer than desired finished length. Knot each end; attach one end to a hook or something similar and twist from the other end until strands are very tight. Fold cord at center and let the strands twist around each other. Knot ends, remove original knots and trim ends.

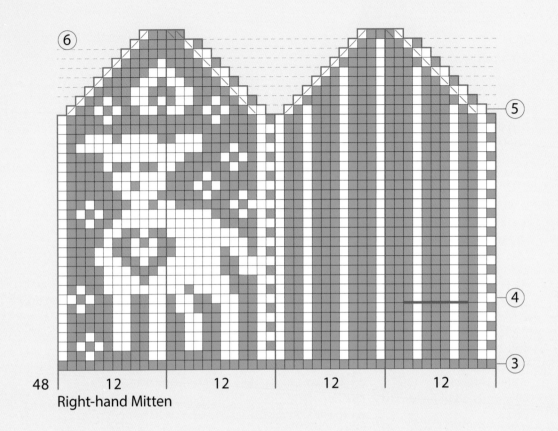

6

5

4

3

48 | 12 | 12 | 12 | 12

Right-hand Mitten

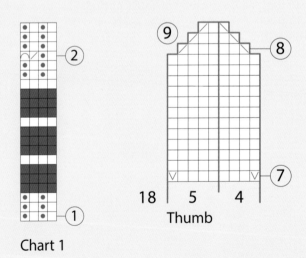

2

1

Chart 1

9

8

7

18 | 5 | 4

Thumb

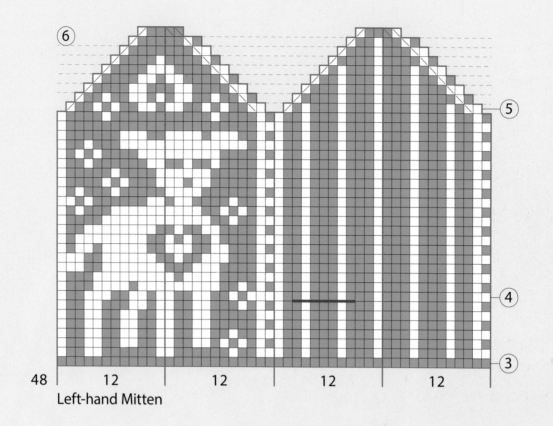

Left-hand Mitten

	Knit
⊙	Purl
⌒	Yarnover
⩒	Increase 1 st
⧅	Right-leaning decrease
⧄	Left-leaning decrease

MOTIFS
WITH
PERSONAL MEANING

Mittens can be a way of telling something about the person who wears them. Maybe you'll find some mittens in this section that describe you well—perhaps you are an angel, rocker, fisher(wo)man, sailor, newly married, or just someone who is happy in the snow! It's always wonderful to be able to give someone mittens that suit the recipient perfectly.

ANGEL MITTENS

MATERIALS
Yarn: CYCA #1 (sock/ fingering/baby) Rauma Finullgarn (100% wool; 191 yd/175 m / 50 g), White #400 and Light Lilac #471
Needles: U.S. size 2.5 / 3 mm, set of 5 dpn

It is good to have an angel on your side. These angel mittens will make a fine gift for someone who is an angel to you—or someone who needs extra angels around them every day.

These mittens have a comfortable fit so they can be worn over or under jacket sleeves as needed.

I recommend that you knit them a little large with a yarn that can be felted.

Instructions

The mittens are knitted the same way except for the placement of the thumbs.

With Light Lilac, CO 60 sts. Divide the sts onto 4 dpn = 15 sts per dpn. Join, being careful not to twist cast-on row.

1) Work following Chart 1 (see page 167), repeating the motifs 4 times around.

2) Continue to the chart for the right- and left-hand mittens (see page 166).

3) **Thumbhole:** The thick line on the chart (blue line for left-hand and red for right) indicates the placement of the thumbhole. Knit the 11 sts for the thumb with a smooth contrast color scrap yarn. Slide the sts back to the left needle and knit in pattern.

4) Continue following the chart up to the encircled 4, and then shape top by decreasing as shown on the chart.

5) When 7 sts each remain on the front and back, seam the sets of stitches with Kitchener st.

6) **Thumb:** Insert a dpn into the sts below the scrap yarn and another dpn into the sts above the scrap yarn. Remove the scrap yarn = 11 + 11 sts. On the first rnd of the thumb, increase to 26 sts total by picking up and knitting 2 sts at each side (see chart).

7) Work thumb to encircled 7 and then shape top as shown on chart.

8) When 6 sts remain, cut yarn and draw end through rem sts. Weave in all yarn ends neatly on WS.

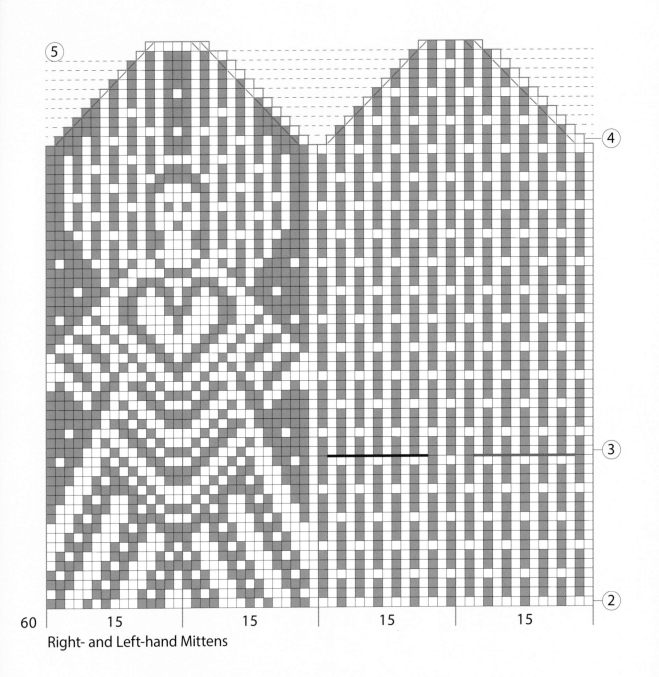

Right- and Left-hand Mittens

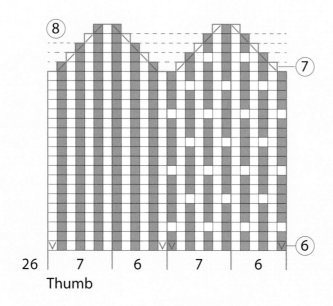

26 | 7 | 6 | 7 | 6

Thumb

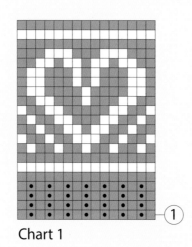

Chart 1

Knit

Purl

Increase 1 st

Right-leaning decrease

Left-leaning decrease

SHIP AHOY!

MATERIALS

Yarn: CYCA #3 (DK/ light worsted) Du Store Alpakka Sterk (40% Merino wool, 40% alpaca, 20% nylon; 150 yd/137 m / 50 g), Navy Blue #815 and White #806 + small amounts of Red #828 and Green #812 for embroidery

Needles: U.S. size 1.5 (2.5) / 2.5 (3) mm, set of 5 dpn (needle sizes in parentheses for larger sizes)

These mittens will keep your hands warm—even when you're out at sea. The Selbu rose, which serves as a compass here, shows north, south, east, and west. The thumbs hold the correct signal light colors for the port and starboard (left and right). The striped cuffs end with a rhomboid and correspond to the stripes on a captain's uniform. These are not mittens for landlubbers!

Instructions

With Navy Blue, CO 60 sts. Divide the sts onto 4 dpn = 15 sts per ndl. Join, being careful not to twist cast-on row. Work 12 rnds of k2, p2 ribbing. Continue ribbing with 3 rnds White, 2 rnds Navy Blue, 3 rnds White, 2 rnds Navy Blue, 3 rnds White. Now work around in stockinette with 2 rnds Navy Blue and 3 rnds White. On the last rnd, increase 1 st on each needle = 64 sts or 16 sts per dpn.

1) Next, work following the charts for the right- and left-hand mittens (see page 170).

2) **Thumbhole:** The thick line on the chart (blue for left-hand, red for right) indicates the placement of the thumbhole. Knit the 12 sts for the thumb with a smooth contrast color scrap yarn. Slide the sts back to the left needle and knit in pattern.

3) From the point marked by an encircled 3, both mittens are worked alike.

4) Continue following the chart up to the encircled 4, and then shape top by decreasing as shown on the chart.

5) When 5 sts each remain on the front and back, seam the sets of sts with Kitchener st.

6) **Thumb:** Insert a dpn into the sts below the scrap yarn and another dpn into the sts above the scrap yarn. Remove the scrap yarn = 12 + 12 sts. On the first rnd of the thumb, increase to 27 sts total by picking up and knitting 2 sts at one side and 1 st at each side (see chart).

7) At the encircled 7 on thumb chart, decrease for the top as shown.

8) When 7 sts remain, cut yarn and draw end through rem sts. Weave in all yarn ends neatly on WS.

9) With Red and Green, using duplicate stitch, embroider the starboard and port signal lights on the thumbs.

Knit
Increase 1 st
Right-leaning decrease
Left-leaning decrease

5

4

3

2

1

64
16   16   16   16   16

Right-hand Mitten

8

7

9

6

Right Thumb   Left Thumb   27   6   7   7   7

Thumb

LET'S ROCK!

MATERIALS

Yarn: CYCA #1 (sock/fingering/baby) Rauma Finullgarn (100% wool; 191 yd/175 m / 50 g), Black #436 and White #400

Needles: U.S. size 2.5 / 3 mm, set of 5 dpn

These mittens were specially designed for rock musicians and their fans. While you knit, imagine the needles are drumsticks and you're listening to some intense music. Maybe these mittens will persuade a tough guy to actually wear something warm on his hands when he goes out. We can only hope!

These mittens have a simple and loose shaping and are easy to knit.

Instructions

The mittens are knitted the same way except for the placement of the thumbs.

With Black, CO 60 sts. Divide the sts onto 4 dpn = 15 sts per dpn. Join, being careful not to twist cast-on row.

1) Work following the chart for the right- and left-hand mittens (see page 174).

2) **Thumbhole:** The thick line on the chart (blue line for left-hand and red for right) indicates the placement of the thumbhole. Knit the 11 sts for the thumb with a smooth contrast color scrap yarn. Slide the sts back to the left needle and knit in pattern.

3) Continue following the chart up to the encircled 3 and then shape top by decreasing as shown on the chart.

4) When 8 sts remain, cut yarn and draw end through rem sts.

5) **Thumb:** Insert a dpn into the sts below the scrap yarn and another dpn into the sts above the scrap yarn. Remove the scrap yarn = 11 + 11 sts. On the first rnd of the thumb, increase to 26 sts total by picking up and knitting 2 sts at each side (see chart).

6) Work thumb to encircled 6, and then shape top as shown on chart.

7) When 6 sts remain, cut yarn and draw end through rem sts. Weave in all yarn ends neatly on WS.

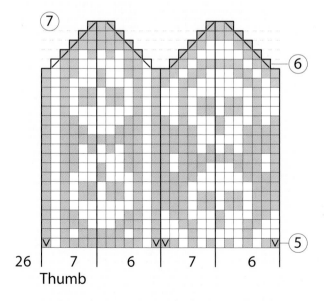

26 | 7 | 6 | 7 | 6

Thumb

		Knit
●	●	Purl
⋁	⋁	Increase 1 st
⟋	⟋	Right-leaning decrease
⟍	⟍	Left-leaning decrease

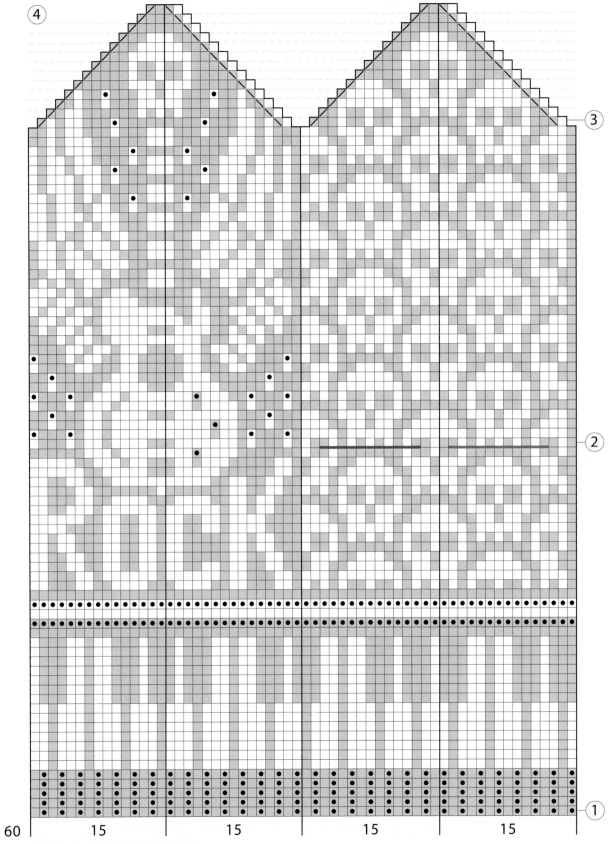

④

③

②

①

60

15　　　　　15　　　　　15　　　　　15

Right- and Left-hand Mittens

FISHERMAN'S FRIEND

MATERIALS

Yarn: CYCA #1 (sock/fingering/baby) Rauma Finullgarn (100% wool; 191 yd/175 m / 50 g), Blue #437 and White #401

Needles: U.S. size 2.5 / 3 mm, set of 5 dpn

These mittens were designed in appreciation of our good friend the codfish. On the front of the mitten, two speckled fish are swimming in the same formation as the fish in the Pisces constellation. The palm of the mitten is meant as a warning that we must take good care of the fish in the sea, because no one can live on dry fish bones—even if they have never been so decorative. These mittens will suit both men and women. They're easy to knit and very stylish!

Instructions

The mittens are knitted the same way except for the placement of the thumbs and a few rows on the center of the mitten, above the thumb. The section that is worked differently on each mitten is marked off by red lines.

With Blue, CO 60 sts. Divide the sts onto 4 dpn = 15 sts per dpn. Join, being careful not to twist cast-on row.

1) Work following Chart 1, repeating the motifs around.

2) Continue to the chart for the right- and left-hand mittens.

3) **NOTE:** The section marked off with red lines on the mitten chart (marked by encircled 4) is for the left hand only. That section is worked from the bottom chart on page 177 for the right hand.

4) **Thumbhole:** The thick line on the left-/right-hand chart indicates the placement of the thumbhole. Knit the 11 sts for the thumb with a smooth contrast color scrap yarn. Slide the sts back to the left needle and knit in pattern.

5) Continue following the chart up to the encircled 5, and then shape top by decreasing as shown on the chart.

6) When 7 sts each remain on the front and back, seam the sets of stitches with Kitchener st.

7) **Thumb:** Insert a dpn into the sts below the scrap yarn and another dpn into the sts above the scrap yarn. Remove the scrap yarn = 11 + 11 sts. On the first rnd of the thumb, increase to 26 sts total by picking up and knitting 2 sts at each side (see chart).

8) Work thumb to the encircled 8, and then shape top as shown on chart.

9) When 6 sts remain, cut yarn and draw end through rem sts. Weave in all yarn ends neatly on WS.

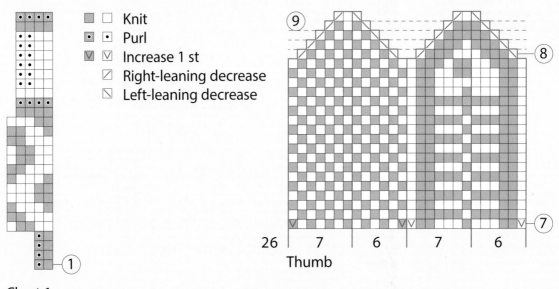

Knit
Purl
Increase 1 st
Right-leaning decrease
Left-leaning decrease

26 · 7 · 6 · 7 · 6

Thumb

Chart 1

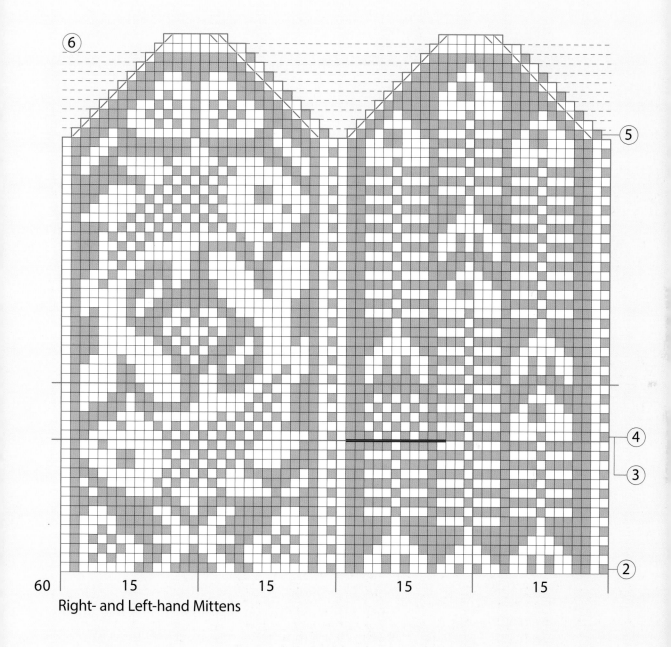

6

5

4

3

2

60   15   15   15   15

Right- and Left-hand Mittens

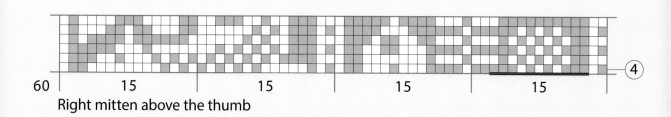

4

60   15   15   15   15

Right mitten above the thumb

BRIDAL PAIR MITTENS

MATERIALS

Women's

Yarn: CYCA #1 (sock/fingering/baby) Rauma Finullgarn (100% wool; 191 yd/175 m / 50 g), Black #436, White #400, and Red #418

Needles: U.S. size 1.5 / 2.5 mm, set of 5 dpn

Men's

Yarn: CYCA #2 (sport/baby) Dale Garn Falk (100% wool; 116 yd/106 m / 50 g), Black #0090, White #0010, and Blue #5545

Needles: U.S. size 2.5 / 3 mm, set of 5 dpn

These are one of the finest presents one could give to a bridal pair or celebrant and should have a prominent place on the gift table. The bride's mittens are luxuriously decorated with patterns inspired by Norwegian folk costumes. The motif with the couple under the Tree of Life is often used in folk art and interpreted as a symbol of fertility. You can knit in the couple's initials and the date on the palm.

A special feature of bridal mittens is the two-end knitted bands. The mittens also have decorative cords that mimic the chevrons on the bands.

Both sizes are knitted from the same pattern; the yarn and needle sizes make the difference.

Instructions

With Red (Blue), CO 64 sts. Divide the sts onto 4 dpn = 16 sts per dpn. Join, being careful not to twist cast-on row.

1) Work following the cuff chart on page 181. The pattern is repeated twice around. Work the blue squares on the chart with Red for the women's size. Begin the cuff with 2 rnds of k1, p1 ribbing as shown on the chart.

2) At the encircled 2 of the cuff chart, work the purl braid. The braid is worked all in purl, alternating the two colors; both strands remain on the RS throughout.

Rnd 1: *Purl 1 st; bring the other color UNDER the yarn just used and purl the next st. Repeat from * around. The yarns will twist around each other as you work but will untwist on the next round. Slide your fingers between the strands to push the twist down the yarn as necessary.

Rnd 2: Alternate the colors (keeping sequence as set) but bring the new yarn OVER the one just used. Every st in the round is purled.

3) Continue following chart to the encircled 3, and then work another purl braid as before.

4) Change to the chart for the right- and left-hand mittens. Right mitten: Cut the White yarn and begin the round on needle 3. This places the two-end purl band on the outer side of the mitten where the cord will be attached.

5) **Thumbhole:** The thick line on the chart (blue line for the left mitten and red for the right) indicates the placement of the thumbhole. Knit the 11 sts for the thumb with a smooth contrast color scrap yarn. Slide the sts back to the left needle and knit in pattern.

6) The center section (marked off with heavy green lines) is worked differently on each mitten. One palm could have a monogram with initials and date. Chart your own design!

7) Continue following the chart up to the encircled 7, and then shape top by decreasing as shown on the chart.

8) When 6 sts remain, cut yarn and draw end through rem sts.

9) **Thumb:** Insert a dpn into the sts below the scrap yarn and another dpn into the sts above the scrap yarn. Remove the scrap yarn = 11 + 11 sts. On the first rnd of the thumb, increase to 26 sts total by picking up and knitting 2 sts at each side (see chart).

10) Work thumb to encircled 10, and then shape top as shown on chart.

11) When 6 sts remain, cut yarn and draw end through rem sts. Weave in all yarn ends neatly on WS.

Decorative Cords: Twist cords with four strands of yarn, 2 strands of White and 2 of Red or Blue. Because the women's mittens are knitted with a finer yarn, use 4 doubled strands. Knot one end and attach to a hook or something similar. Braid the strands, alternating colors. Grab the strand at outermost left and braid to the right; bring the yarn under the two next strands, and over the last. Braid the same way, alternating colors, until cord is desired length. Tie a knot at both ends. Sew the center of the cord at the side by the top purl braid on each mitten; knot

64

16 16 16 16

Right- and Left-hand Mittens

			Knit
		•	Purl
		⩔	Increase 1 st
		⟋	Right-leaning decrease
		⟍	Left-leaning decrease

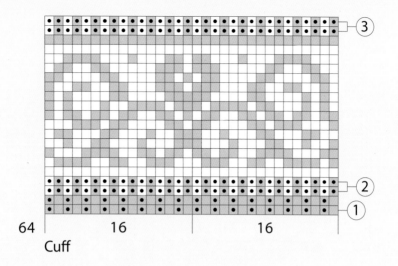

64   16   16

Cuff

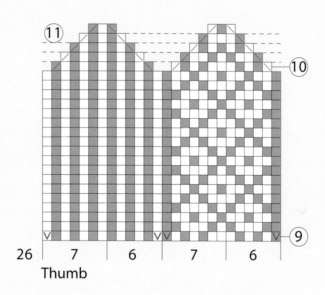

26   7   6   7   6

Thumb

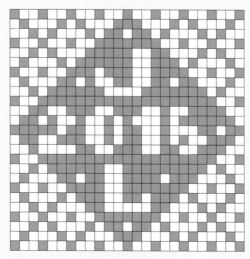

Monogram (example)

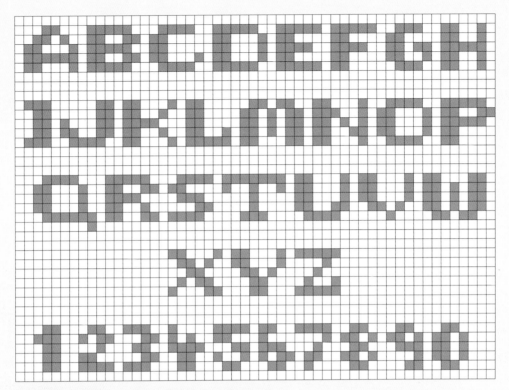

Alphabet and numbers for the monogram

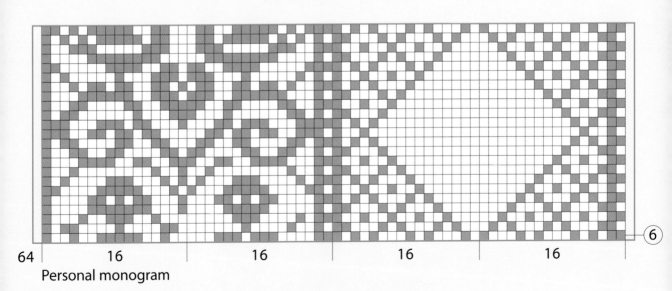

6

64   16   16   16   16

Personal monogram

The photo shows mittens with the Norwegian lyrics; the chart has been updated with English.

TIDDELY POM

MATERIALS

Yarn: CYCA #1 (sock/fingering/baby) Rauma Finullgarn (100% wool; 191 yd/175 m / 50 g), left-over amounts of White #0010, Blue #5545, Eggplant #5052, Pink #4203, and Green #8426

Needles: U.S. size 1.5 / 2.5 mm, set of 5 dpn

These mittens are for everyone who loves snow and doesn't turn sour-faced when the first snow falls—quite the opposite, in fact. You might even break out in Winnie-the-Pooh's little tune, happily proclaiming that winter is finally here!

These mittens are easy to knit and great to have on your hands if you like to play in the snow. You can use any selection of colors and yarns from your stash basket; those listed are just suggestions. Do make sure that the yarns are the same thickness and quality. Only one yarn is used for the thumb, and it can be thinner than the others. You might also want to draw your own pattern with several colors and chart it.

and trim for a little tassel at the end.

Instructions

With White, CO 60 sts. Knit 4 rows back and forth and then divide the sts onto 4 dpn = 15 sts per dpn. Join, being careful not to twist.

1) Work following Chart 1 on page 186. The motifs are repeated around.

2) Continue to the chart for the right- and left-hand mittens.

3) **Thumbhole:** The thick line on the chart (blue line for the left mitten and red for the right) indicates the placement of the thumbhole. Knit the 11 sts for the thumb with a smooth contrast color scrap yarn. Slide the sts back to the left needle and knit in pattern.

4) The lower section (marked off with red lines and indicated by encircled 4) is worked differently on each mitten. The chart for this section of the right mitten is on page 187.

5) At the chart row marked by an encircled 5, continue both mittens the same way.

6) Continue following the chart up to the encircled 6, and then shape top by decreasing as shown on the chart.

7) When 8 sts remain, cut yarn and draw end through rem sts.

8) **Thumb:** Insert a dpn into the sts below the scrap yarn and another dpn into the sts above the scrap yarn. Remove the scrap yarn = 11 + 11 sts. On the first rnd of the thumb, increase to 24 sts total by picking up and knitting 1 st at each side (see chart).

9) Work thumb to encircled 9 and then shape top as shown on chart.

10) When 6 sts remain, cut yarn and draw end through rem sts.

Seam the garter stitch section at lower edge of each mitten. Weave in all yarn ends neatly on WS.

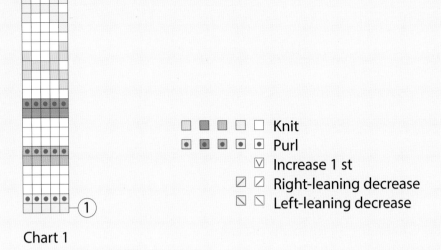

Knit
Purl
Increase 1 st
Right-leaning decrease
Left-leaning decrease

Chart 1

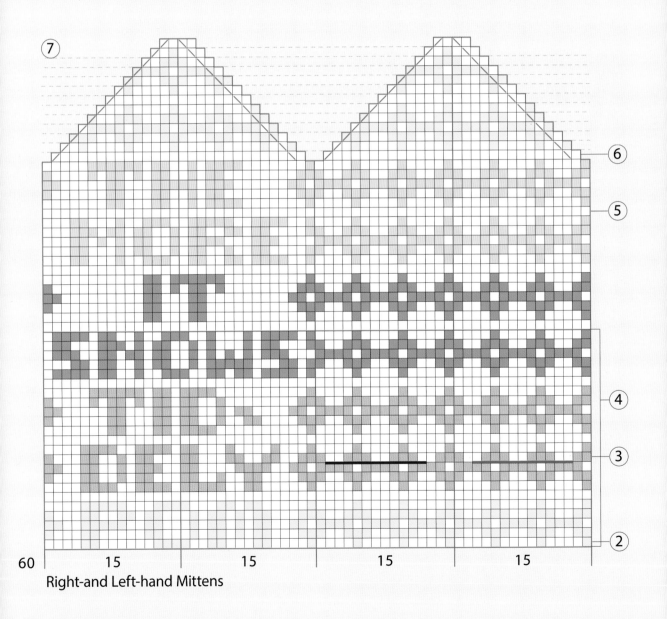

60   15   15   15   15

Right-and Left-hand Mittens

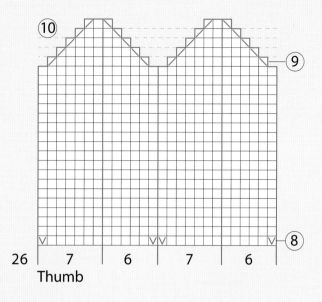

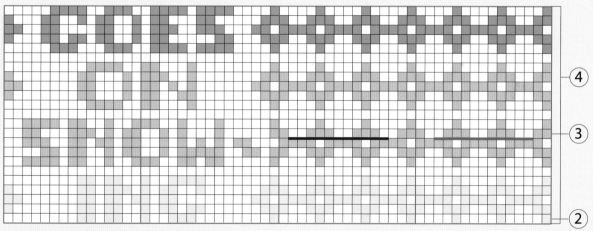

Right-hand Mitten, text

EXOTIC MITTENS

In the southern latitudes, we find animals with astonishing appearances and charming patterns in their coats. In those warm climates, knitted mittens aren't quite so necessary, but why not adapt these pretty creatures for your own style of Norwegian mitten? It was just too tempting to play with these patterns and colors, so four animals from the southern hemisphere have been given their own designs.

ZEBRA MITTENS

MATERIALS

Yarn: CYCA #1 (sock/ fingering/baby) Dale Garn Daletta (100% wool; 153 yd/140 m / 50 g), White #0010, Black #0090, and Orange #2827

Needles: U.S. size 2.5 / 3 mm, set of 5 dpn

A zebra is wrapped around each mitten. The stripes in his pelt stand out like a three-dimensional twist against the striped background. The theme is "contrast." The black and white stripes of the zebra visually contrast against the leopard's black spots on the orange background.

Instructions

Both mittens are worked the same way except for the placement of the thumb.

With Black, CO 62 sts. Divide the sts onto 4 dpn. Join, being careful not to twist cast-on row.

1) Work following Chart 1 (see page 193), repeating the motifs around.

2) At the chart row marked by an encircled 2, increase 1 st on each needle = 66 sts total.

3) After completing Chart 1, work following the chart for the right- and left-hand mittens (see page 192). On the first round, decrease 2 sts as shown on the chart. For the rest of the mitten, hold the yarns with the White as dominant.

4) **Thumbhole:** The thick line on the chart indicates the placement of the thumbhole (blue line for left-hand mitten and red line for right mitten). Knit the 12 sts for the thumb with a smooth contrast color scrap yarn. Slide the sts back to the left needle and knit in pattern.

5) Continue following the chart up to the encircled 5, and then shape top by decreasing as shown on the chart.

6) When 6 sts each remain on the front and back, cut yarn and draw end through rem 12 sts.

7) **Thumb:** Insert a dpn into the sts below the scrap yarn and another dpn into the sts above the scrap yarn. Remove the scrap yarn = 12 + 12 sts. On the first rnd of the thumb, increase to 28 sts total by picking up and knitting 2 sts at each side (see chart). Work the chart twice for each round. The front and back of the thumbs are alike.

8) Work thumb to encircled 8, and then shape top as shown on chart.

9) When 8 sts remain, cut yarn and draw end through rem sts. Weave in all yarn ends neatly on WS.

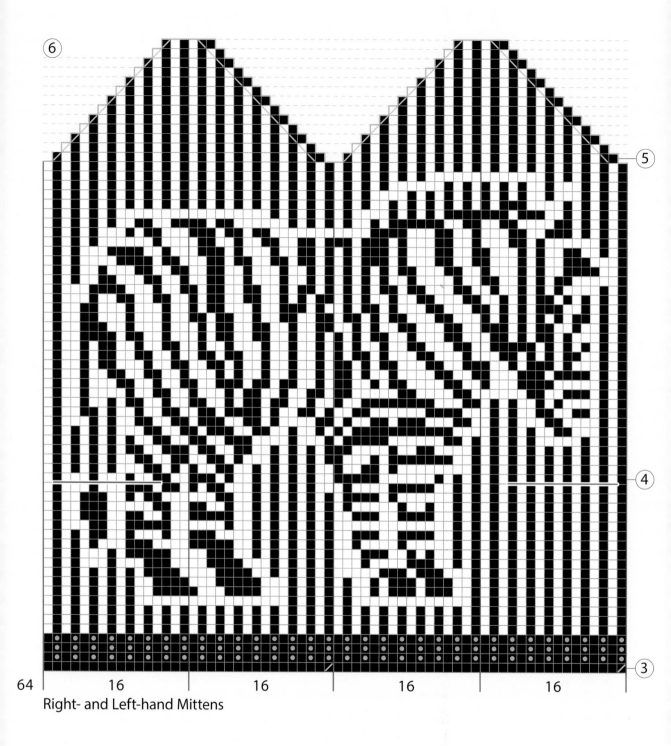

Right- and Left-hand Mittens

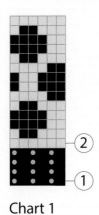

Chart 1

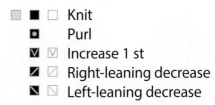

- Knit
- Purl
- Increase 1 st
- Right-leaning decrease
- Left-leaning decrease

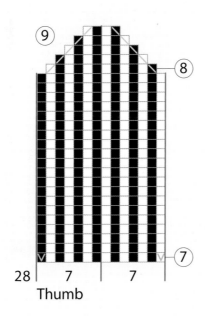

28 | 7 | 7

Thumb

TIGER CUB

MATERIALS

These mittens can be knitted in two sizes; the small ones will fit infants up to 1½ years old. The thumb can be omitted on mittens for the smallest children.

Yarn: CYCA #1 (sock/fingering/baby) Rauma Garn Baby Panda (100% Merino wool; 191 yd/175 m / 50 g), Orange #157 and Black #36

Needles: U.S. size 1.5 / 2.5 mm, set of 5 dpn

The larger size mittens will fit children about 7 years old

Yarn: CYCA #2 (sport/baby) Dale Garn Falk (100% wool; 116 yd/106 m / 50 g), Orange #3418 and Black #0090

Needles: U.S. size 2.5 / 3 mm, set of 5 dpn

It's small, soft, and sweet. It pats at you delightfully with its soft paws—but a moment later it springs up, snarls, and growls. If you know a child with similar characteristics, yes, you will also recognize a real tiger cub.

These sweet children's mittens can be knitted in several sizes following the same pattern, depending on your choice of yarn and needle sizes.

Instructions

Both mittens are knitted the same way except for the placement of the thumb.

With Orange, CO 44 sts. Divide the sts evenly onto 4 dpn (= 11 sts per ndl). Join, being careful not to twist cast-on row.

1) Begin with k2/p2 ribbing around as shown on the ribbing chart below. Change colors as shown on the charts.

2) After completing the ribbing, work following the chart for the right- and left-hand mittens (see page 196). On the first round, increase a total of 4 sts as shown on the chart = 48 sts.

3) **Thumbhole:** The thick line on the chart indicates the placement of the thumbhole (blue line for left-hand mitten and red line for right mitten). Knit the 8 sts for the thumb with a smooth contrast color scrap yarn. Slide the sts back to the left needle and knit in pattern.

4) Continue following the chart up to the encircled 4, and then shape top by decreasing as shown on the chart.

5) When 4 sts each remain on the front and back, cut yarn and draw end through rem sts.

6) **Thumb:** Insert a dpn into the sts below the scrap yarn and another dpn into the sts above the scrap yarn. Remove the scrap yarn = 8 + 8 sts. On the first rnd of the thumb, increase to 18 sts total by picking up and knitting 1 st at each side (see chart).

7) Work thumb to encircled 7, and then shape top as shown on chart.

8) When 6 sts remain, cut yarn and draw end through rem sts. Weave in all yarn ends neatly on WS.

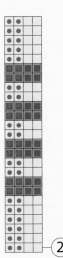

2

Left-leaning decrease

▨	☐	Knit
▨	⊡	Purl
☒	☑	Increase 1 st
◪	◩	Right-leaning decrease
◣	◥	Ribbing

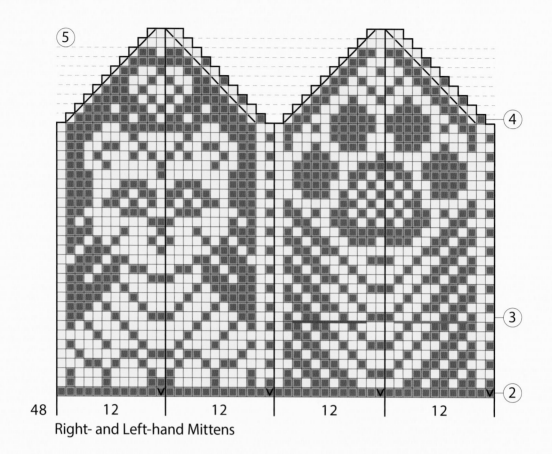

⑤

④

③

②

| 48 | 12 | 12 | 12 | 12 |

Right- and Left-hand Mittens

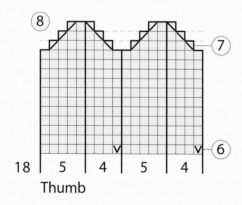

⑧

⑦

⑥

| 18 | 5 | 4 | 5 | 4 |

Thumb

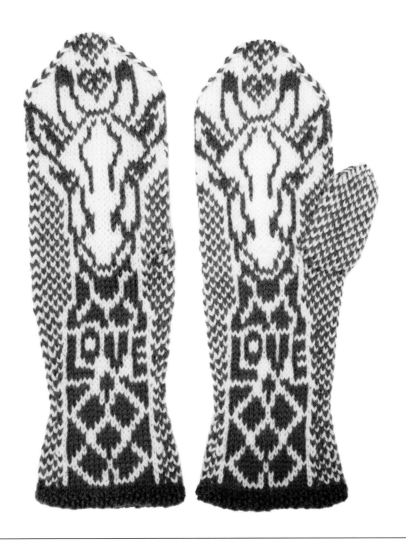

GIRAFFE

MATERIALS
Yarn: CYCA #1 (sock/
fingering/baby) Dale
Garn Daletta (100% wool;
153 yd/140 m / 50 g),
Dark Taupe #2671 and
Natural White #0020
Needles: U.S. size 2.5 /
3 mm, set of 5 dpn

The giraffe is long and lovely, just like these
mittens. Our giraffe bears an inviting mes-
sage: LOVE. With wishes for long-lasting
love! The tapered sides mean that the mittens will fit your hand well.

Instructions

Both mittens are worked the same way except for the placement of the thumb. The thumbs are placed so that the giraffe turns its face outward on one mitten and inward on the other.

With Brown, CO 60 sts. Divide the sts onto 4 dpn = 15 sts per ndl. Join, being careful not to twist cast-on row.

1) Work following the chart for the right- and left-hand mittens.

2) At each of the chart rows marked by an encircled 2, decrease 1 st on each needle as shown = 48 sts total.

3) On each of the chart rows marked by an encircled 3, increase 1 st on each needle as shown = 60 sts.

4) **Thumbhole:** The thick line on the chart (blue for left mitten and red for right) indicates the placement of the thumbhole. Knit the 11 sts for the thumb with a smooth contrast color scrap yarn. Slide the sts back to the left needle and knit in pattern.

5) Continue following the chart up to the encircled 5, and then shape top by decreasing as shown on the chart.

6) When 7 sts each remain on the front and back, seam the sets of sts with Kitchener st.

7) **Thumb:** Insert a dpn into the sts below the scrap yarn and another dpn into the sts above the scrap yarn. Remove the scrap yarn = 11 + 11 sts. On the first rnd of the thumb, increase to 26 sts total by picking up and knitting 2 sts at each side (see chart).

8) Work thumb to encircled 8, and then shape top as shown on chart.

9) When 6 sts remain, cut yarn and draw end through rem sts. Weave in all yarn ends neatly on WS.

☐ ☒ Knit
   ☒ Purl
☑ ☑ Increase 1 st
☒ ☒ Right-leaning decrease
☒ ☒ Left-leaning decrease

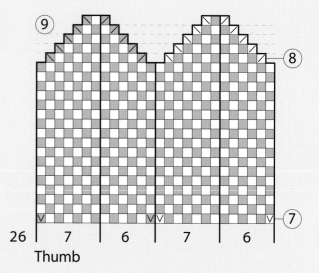

26 | 7 | 6 | 7 | 6

Thumb

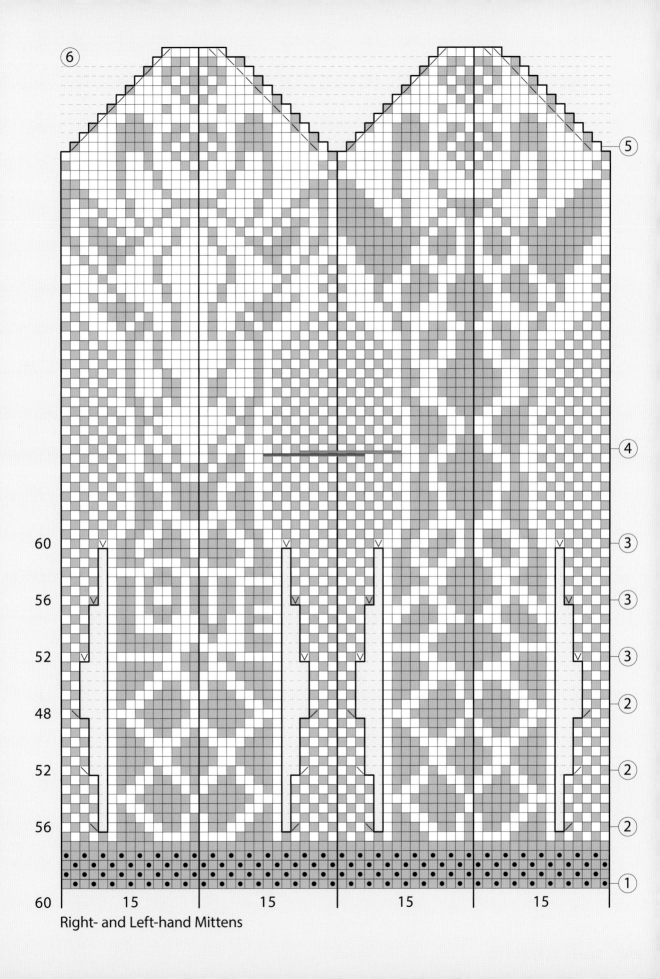

Right- and Left-hand Mittens

TANGO ELEPHANTS

MATERIALS
Yarn: CYCA #1 (sock/fingering/baby) Sandnes Garn Sisu (80% wool, 20% nylon; 191 yd/175 m / 50 g), White #1001 and Light Blue #5930
Needles: U.S. size 2.5 / 3 mm, set of 5 dpn

Elephants aren't clumsy at all, but rather quite elegant when they sway together in a delightful tango. When they've danced themselves onto the palm of the mitten, they sneak a quick kiss with their trunks.

Instructions

Both mittens are worked the same way except for the placement of the thumbs.

1) With White, CO 56 sts. Divide the sts evenly onto 4 dpn (= 14 sts per ndl). Join, being careful not to twist cast-on row. Work following the chart for the right- and left-hand mittens (see page 202).

2) At the chart row marked with an encircled 2, increase 1 st on each needle as shown = 60 sts.

3) **Thumbhole:** The thick line on the chart (blue for left mitten and red for right) indicates the placement of the thumbhole. Knit the 11 sts for the thumb with a smooth contrast color scrap yarn. Slide the sts back to the left needle and knit in pattern.

4) Continue following the chart up to the encircled 4, and then shape top by decreasing as shown on the chart.

5 When 7 sts each remain on the front and back, seam the sets of stitches with Kitchener stitch.

6) **Thumb:** Insert a dpn into the sts below the scrap yarn and another dpn into the sts above the scrap yarn. Remove the scrap yarn = 11 + 11 sts. On the first rnd of the thumb, increase to 26 sts total by picking up and knitting 2 sts at each side (see chart).

7) Work thumb in pattern to chart row marked by an encircled 7 and then shape top as shown.

8) When 6 sts remain, cut yarn and draw end through rem sts. Weave in all yarn ends neatly on WS.

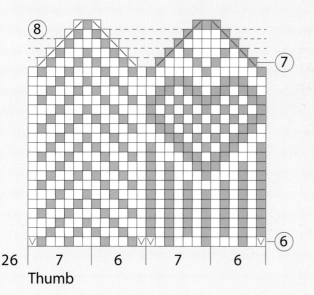

■	□	Knit
	⊡	Purl
	☑	Increase 1 st
▧	◩	Right-leaning decrease
◤	��	Left-leaning decrease

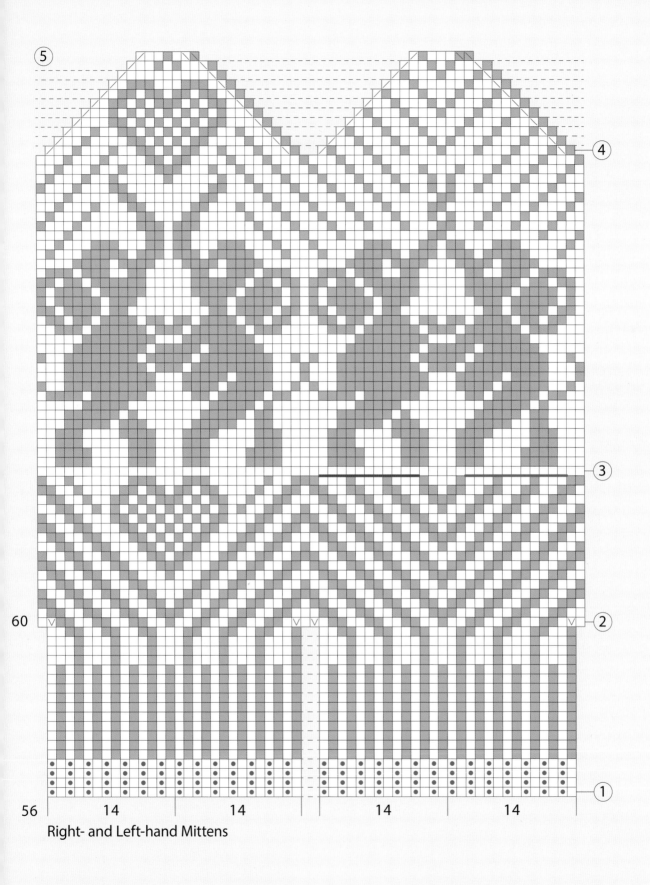

Right- and Left-hand Mittens

BABY ELEPHANT

MATERIALS
Yarn: CYCA #2 (sport/ baby) Dale Garn Falk (100% wool; 116 yd/106 m / 50 g), White #0010 and Soft Blue #5943
Needles: U.S. size 2.5 / 3 mm, set of 5 dpn
Size: Child, approx. 5-7 years

Little elephants like water and love to take quick baths. Many human babies also love to splash in the water (and the mud). With good, warm wool mittens on their hands, their fingers won't get cold even when they're wet.

These mittens would be especially sweet in pink and white. Who hasn't thought of pink elephants?

Instructions

Both mittens are knitted the same way except for the placement of the thumb.

With White, CO 48 sts. Divide the sts evenly onto 4 dpn (= 12 sts per ndl). Join, being careful not to twist cast-on row.

1) Work following the chart for the right- and left-hand mittens. Repeat the chart row marked by encircled 1 3 times (= 3 rnds k1, p1 ribbing).

2) Next, repeat the chart row marked by an encircled 2 6 times (= 6 rnds of k1 Blue, p1 White).

3) Repeat the chart row marked by an encircled 3 12 times (= 12 rnds of k1 Blue, k1 White).

4) **Thumbhole:** The thick line on the chart indicates the placement of the thumbhole (blue line for left-hand mitten and red line for right mitten). Knit the 7 sts for the thumb with a smooth contrast color scrap yarn. Slide the sts back to the left needle and knit in pattern.

5) Continue following the chart up to the encircled 5, and then shape top by decreasing as shown on the chart.

6) When 5 sts each remain on the front and back, seam sets of sts with Kitchener st.

7) **Thumb:** The thumb is rather tightly knitted in pattern so I recommend going up a needle size so the thumb won't be too tight. Insert a dpn into the sts below the scrap yarn and another dpn into the sts above the scrap yarn. Remove the scrap yarn = 7 + 7 sts. On the first rnd of the thumb, increase to 18 sts total by picking up and knitting 2 sts at each side (see chart).

8) Work thumb to encircled 8, and then shape top as shown on chart.

9) When 6 sts remain, cut yarn and draw end through rem sts. Weave in all yarn ends neatly on WS.

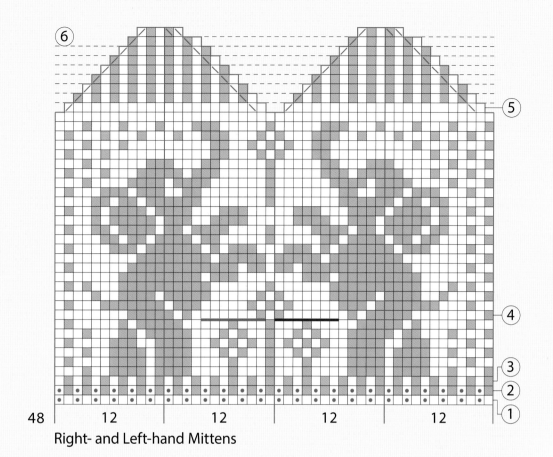

48 | 12 | 12 | 12 | 12

Right- and Left-hand Mittens

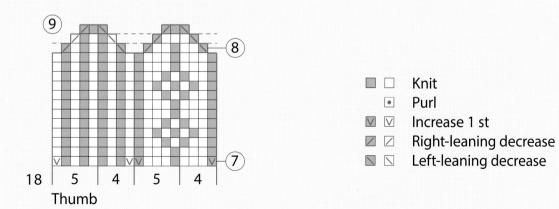

18 | 5 | 4 | 5 | 4

Thumb

		Knit
	⦁	Purl
		Increase 1 st
		Right-leaning decrease
		Left-leaning decrease

YOUR OWN DESIGN

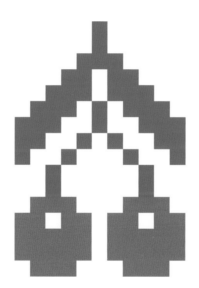

MAKE YOUR OWN MITTEN PATTERNS

The schematic is the same as for the rocker, cat, and dog mittens. If you want mittens with a ribbed cuff, begin the pattern motif(s) at the red horizontal line on the mitten hand.

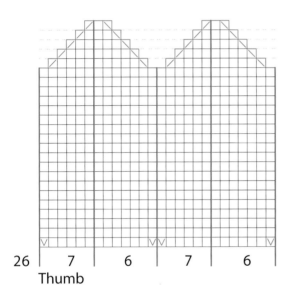

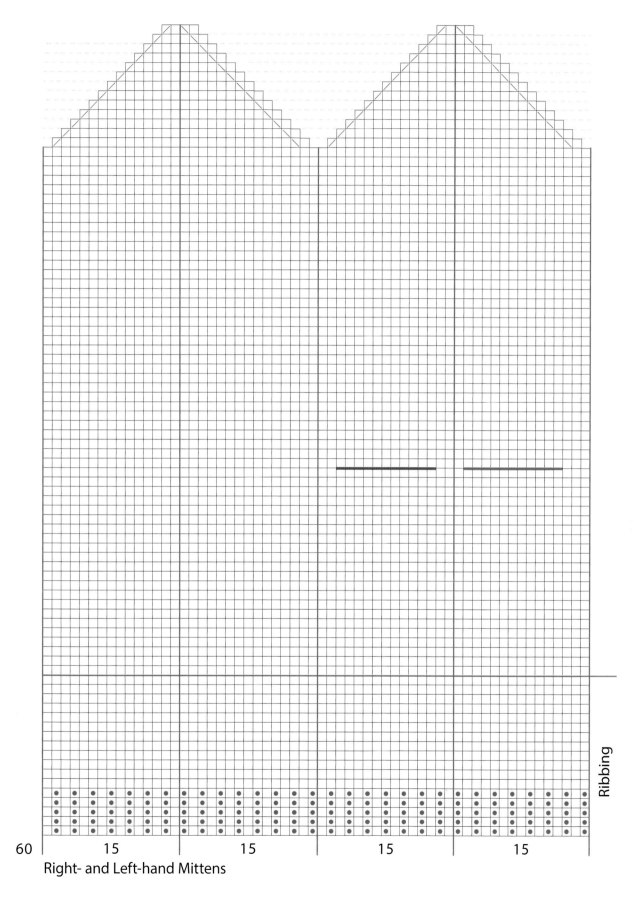

60   15   15   15   15

Right- and Left-hand Mittens

Ribbing

DESIGN YOUR OWN CHILDREN'S MITTENS

You can develop your creativity here and design patterns for special children's mittens.

The schematic is the same as for the little fox mittens. The pattern motif for the mitten begins above the ribbed cuff. CO 44 sts and work 16 rounds of ribbing. After completing the ribbing, increase to 48 sts per round.

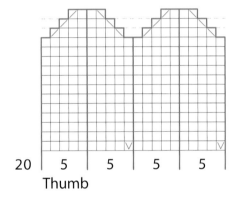

20 | 5 | 5 | 5 | 5
Thumb

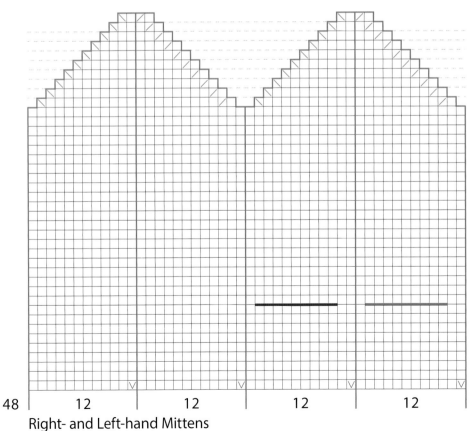

48 | 12 | 12 | 12 | 12
Right- and Left-hand Mittens

YOUR NOTES

Always write down what you've done as you knit—the yarn and needles you used and the results. Good notes are worth their weight in gold!

NAME PANELS

You can add a name panel to almost any pattern in this book, placing it, for example, above the ribbing. The alphabet and number chart here should help you design your own panel. Use the large letters for short names and monograms and the small letters for longer names. The numbers can be used for dates. Make the mittens especially personal!

The date and initials can also be embroidered on with duplicate stitch on an "empty" space of the mittens.

Use these charts to design panels for mittens with 48, 60, 64, or 68 stitches around.

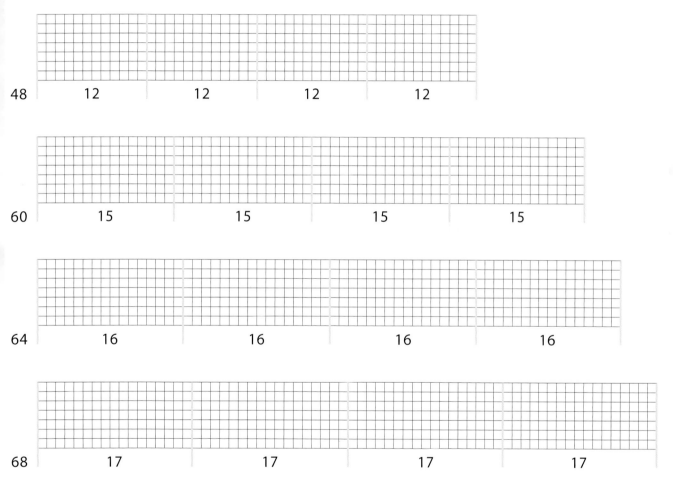

48   12   12   12   12

60   15   15   15   15

64   16   16   16   16

68   17   17   17   17

YARN SUPPLIERS

Dale Garn North America
www.dalegarnnorthamerica.com

Nordic Fiber Arts
www.nordicfiberarts.com

Swedish Yarn Imports
www.swedishyarn.com

Webs – America's Yarn Store
75 Service Center Road
Northampton, M A 01060
800-367-9327
www.yarn.com
customerservice@yarn.com

LoveKnitting.com
www.loveknitting.com/us

If you are unable to obtain any of the yarn used in this book, it can be replaced with a yarn of a similar weight and composition. Please note, however, the finished projects may vary slightly from those shown, depending on the yarn used. Try www.yarnsub.com for suggestions.

   For more information on selecting or substituting yarn, contact your local yarn shop or an online store; they are familiar with all types of yarns and would be happy to help you. Additionally, the online knitting community at Ravelry.com has forums where you can post questions about specific yarns. Yarns come and go so quickly these days and there are so many beautiful yarns available.